叙事诗

NARRATIVE POEM

Yang Lian was one of the original Misty Poets who reacted against the strictures of the Cultural Revolution. Born in Switzerland, the son of a diplomat, he grew up in Beijing and began writing when he was sent to the countryside in the 1970s. On his return he joined the influential literary magazine *Jintian* (Today). His work was criticised in China in 1983 and formally banned in 1989 when he organised memorial services for the dead of Tiananmen while in New Zealand. He was a Chinese poet in exile from 1989 to 1995, lived in London from 1997, and currently lives in Berlin. Translations of his poetry include four collections with Bloodaxe, *Where the Sea Stands Still* (1999), *Concentric Circles* (2005), *Lee Valley Poems* (2009) and *Narrative Poem* (2017), as well as his long poem *Yi* (Green Integer, USA, 2002) and *Riding Pisces: Poems from Five Collections* (Shearsman, 2008), a compilation of earlier work. He is co-editor with W.N. Herbert of *Jade Ladder: Contemporary Chinese Poetry* (Bloodaxe Books, 2012), and was awarded the International Nonino Prize in 2012. Both *Where the Sea Stands Still* and *Narrative Poem* are Poetry Book Society Recommended Translations.

Brian Holton was born in Galashiels in the Scottish Border country but grew up partly in Nigeria. He was the son of an Irish father who was bilingual in English and French, fluent in Hausa and West African Pidgin and competent in Yoruba. After being educated in Greek, French and Latin, he studied Chinese at the universities of Edinburgh and Durham and was the first Programme Director of the Chinese-English/English-Chinese translation programme at Newcastle University, after which he taught translation for ten years at the Hong Kong Polytechnic University. In 1992 he began a continuing working relationship with Yang Lian, which has so far resulted in a dozen books of translated poetry, including *Where the Sea Stands Still* (1999), *Concentric Circles*, with Agnes Hung-Chong Chan (2005), *Lee Valley Poems*, with Agnes Hung-Chong Chan and seven poets (2009), and *Narrative Poem* (2017), all from Bloodaxe. He is the lead translator and associate editor of *Jade Ladder: Contemporary Chinese Poetry* (Bloodaxe Books, 2012). He also translates into Scots and is the only currently-publishing Chinese-Scots translator in the world.

杨炼
YANG LIAN

叙事诗
NARRATIVE POEM

translated by
BRIAN HOLTON

BLOODAXE BOOKS

ISBN: 978 1 78037 351 5

First published 2017 by
Bloodaxe Books Ltd,
Eastburn,
South Park,
Hexham,
Northumberland NE46 1BS

www.bloodaxebooks.com
For further information about Bloodaxe titles
please visit our website or write to
the above address for a catalogue.

This book has been selected to receive financial assistance from English PEN's
PEN Translates programme, supported by Arts Council England. English PEN
exists to promote literature and our understanding of it, to uphold writers'
freedoms around the world, to campaign against the persecution and imprisonment
of writers for stating their views, and to promote the friendly co-operation of writers
and the free exchange of ideas. www.englishpen.org [see also page 268]

Cover design: Neil Astley & Pamela Robertson-Pearce.

Printed in Great Britain by Bell & Bain Limited, Glasgow, Scotland, on
acid-free paper sourced from mills with FSC chain of custody certification.

CONTENTS

第二部 | PART 2
水薄荷哀歌：无时间的现实 | WATERMINT ELEGY: TIMELESS REALITY
（极慢的慢板） | (*Adagio pianissimo*)

第三部 | **PART 3**
哲人之墟：共时·无梦 | RUIN OF SAGES.SYNCHRONIC.DREAMLESS
（小快板 | (*Allegretto*)

叙事诗

NARRATIVE POEM

家风

——《叙事诗》序

２０１０年３月，大陆诗人张枣辞世，他早夭的才华令人
扼腕，作为这一代中，首位病逝而不曾死于非命者，使他
有别于海子、顾城，少了特定的戏剧性，却突显出命运的
苍茫无常。我无意加入挽歌合唱，因为我给他（当然也给
我自己）的小小挽歌，早在２００２年初春就写好了。那
首诗题为《洪荒时代》，写于我们邂逅巴黎，彻夜漫步美
丽空寂的街头，畅谈家世诗事，次晨登车各奔东西之后。
这首诗里，有谶语"写得好　就写至阴暗生命的报复"，也
不乏赞词"有鹤的家风　就出一张鱼的牌吧"＊。我自己尤
喜后一句。"家风"一词，阔别久矣！我欣赏这词的典型汉
语组合，其中二字"家"与"风"，纯然是两个独立意象，并
无必然联系，却天衣无缝地合为一个想象空间。配登堂入
室之风，是什么"风"？细思之，除人品美德之风外，焉有
其它？噫，此风非吾家传，实传吾家也！由是，此风之起，
与青萍之末无涉，却自血脉之初、家学之远，鼓荡而来，
浩浩渺渺，拂入当下。其显形，一见于处世态度，二证之
品味高低。所谓高贵高雅（乃至高傲），无关文采修饰，
端赖此渊源深远的风骨精神。屈原从"帝高阳之苗裔兮"，
歌至他自己的"内美"，正合此意。即或，有形之"鹤的家
风"，在二十世纪大陆政治动荡中屡遭贬低摧毁，我也相
信，无形之"鹤的家风"，仍延续在孑然个人的心中，一度
形同断绝，只要人在，我们也能重新发明它，犹如从汉字
本质中，重新发明整个中文诗学美学传统。读到这首诗，
张枣颇兴奋，说"一定好好写首诗和你！"直到他去世后，
我才听说他绝命前那些"鹤"诗，个中是否相关？我不知道。
但可以肯定，一缕"家风"，是吹到他了。

为《叙事诗》作序而肆言"家风"，似有离题之嫌。碰到较
真的，或许还会问，这是否还魂的"出身论"？我得明言，

11

家风确实和一个社会的等级有关，但等级不等于阶级，特别是我们被灌输太久、浑浑噩噩盲目接受的"阶级"理论，以及被铐锁在新种姓制度里、非拼个你死我活不可的"阶级斗争"。传统中国乡绅社会语境中，"家风"与其说基于财产，不如说源于一代代递增深化的教养和修养，也因此，它先天不信任各种暴发户，却宁肯把价值的尺度交给陶渊明、曹雪芹，你说这些穷死的大诗人是什么阶级？一个金钱的下下者，何妨作精神的上上人？渗透自传因素的《叙事诗》里，我爸爸是一个重要人物。有个当年发生在他身上的故事：我爸爸出身富有，家里拥有吉祥戏院等产业，他由迷昆曲而转向西方古典音乐，到大学毕业时，已对西方经典音乐作品耳熟能详。四九年后出任驻瑞士外交官的六年，更让他用欧洲生活文化，印证了音乐中浸染的人性之美。但文革开始，贝多芬被当作"资产阶级文化的代表"痛加批判。我爸爸面临一个痛苦的抉择：作为中国党员，他应该绝对相信组织；但作为人，他又能清清楚楚感受到，那音乐中充满了爱和美。于是，究竟应当服从谁？这个今天简单得不像问题的问题，当时却不可思议的沉重。倘若肯定自己的感觉，那又该如何判断当初背叛自己家庭、半生奋斗的道路、和曾被美妙许诺的中国未来？所幸的是，他毕竟是我父亲，虽然内心折磨，但他终于选择了美。他认定，美没有错，错的是批判者。很久以后，当我听到这件事，才懂得了，尽管窗外充斥着急风暴雨，但我家的小气候何以能保持人性和爱，并让我相对心智健全地长大？我敬佩的，不是他认定贝多芬，而是这"认定"本身体现了一种从人性出发，重新审视历史的力量。因此，我心服口服地在《叙事诗》（《故乡哀歌》）中写道："绕过星空朝父亲漫步／还原为寓意本身"。

《叙事诗》的写作，从２００５到２００９历时四年多。这是迄今为止，我思想上、诗学上的集大成之作。某种意义上，它把我此前的全部作品，变成了一种初稿、一个进化过程。我指的是，由长诗《 》归纳的"中国手稿"阶段，由组诗《大海停止之处》代表的"南太平洋手稿"阶段，和

12

比经济危机深刻得多的人类思想危机，在渴求诗歌杰作。熔铸"镇国之宝"，当此时也。这，正是当代中文诗最根本的诗意。

《叙事诗》是一首长诗。它和我此前的两部长诗《 》与《同心圆》潜在关联，构成了一种正、反、合的关系。确切地说，中国——外国——中外合一。《 》植根于《易经》象征体系，又敞开于当代中国经验，以七种不同形式的诗、三种不同风格的散文，完成了一场大规模语言试验。诗歌一如诗人自己，"以死亡的形式诞生才真的诞生"。《同心圆》以漂泊经验为底蕴，横跨中、外文化，用一个贯穿的空间意识，组合起五个层层漾开（层层深化？）的同心圆，那个结构，与其说是诗学的，毋宁说更是哲学的，它把时间纳入空间，把自我置于圆心处提问者的位置，最终，思想同心圆取代了线性的进化论，建立起"再被古老的背叛所感动"的思维模式。当代中文的独特语境，使我们的作品必然兼具两大特点：观念性和实验性。即使仅仅写一行诗，我们也得重组古今中外的所有资源。没有这个潜在的大海，漂浮在白纸上的句子就不配称为"诗"。同理，长诗不仅意味着长度。"长"，必须吻合于"深"，又因为要表达那"深"，而非创"新"不可。因此，我读一首长诗，首先希望读到作者臻于完整的人生经验，其次，从中提炼哲学诗学思想的能力，最后才是这件作品的完成度。不得不承认，深度就是难度。在急功近利的当下中国，诗人要么滞留于长满老年斑的"青春期"，没完没了重复原始发泄，要么浅尝辄止，在批发的写作数量和贫瘠的诗歌质量间，表现出吓人的反差。但其实，玩"先锋"不难，而成为有后劲发展出不同写作阶段的"后锋"很难。诗是"欲速则不达"的最佳注解。我写《 》用了五年，《同心圆》四年，现在《叙事诗》又是四年多。三部长诗，十三年以上的生命心血，一种刻意的慢，回顾中才见出航速，结果反而快了。回到我爸爸的人生名言，凡事第一须"自得其乐"，第二须"慢慢来"。这两句话也堪称最佳"写作学"。写即悟道、即修炼，原非人造诗，从来诗造人。诗之文火，幽幽远远，

13

由长诗《同心圆》开始的"欧洲手稿"阶段，以及这些大作品之间，被我称为一个个"思想——艺术项目"的单独诗集。和以前的作品相比，《叙事诗》的难度，在于最具独创性的诗，又必须经受最普遍的公共历史经验的检验。叙一人一家之事，而穿透这个"命运之点"，涵括二十世纪中国复杂的现实、文化、以至文学沧桑。概括成两句话就是：大历史如何缠结个人命运；个人内心又如何构成历史的深度。当每个人都是历史的隐喻，这首"诗"指向的，就是"叙"人类根本处境之"事"。因此，标题《叙事诗》，全然是个思想指向。它的结构中，又隐然渗透着"家风"的传承：当我构思《叙事诗》时，偶然听到英国现代作曲家本杰明·布列顿的三首大提琴组曲，其幽深迂回、一唱三叹，虽然音色现代，但在精神底蕴上，直追德国作曲家巴赫著名的六首大提琴组曲。事后才知道，布列顿这些作品，当年正是为应和巴赫而作。二十世纪最伟大的大提琴演奏家巴勃罗·卡萨尔斯，据说曾演练这六首巴赫组曲十二年之久，一旦演出，早已枯藤倒挂、铅华褪尽，那种深不可测，岂止令人喜爱？直是逼人胆寒！我爸爸自五十年代初，已全心倾慕卡萨尔斯的演奏，尤其百听不厌他的巴赫大提琴组曲。但或许他出于谨慎、或许他自己也不知道其人的另一壮举：从１９３７年到１９５５年，为抗议西班牙佛朗哥的独裁统治，卡萨尔斯拒绝到任何纳粹、独裁或"观点不清"的国家演出。就是说，在这部分世界上，他整整沉默了十八年。这最深的沉默，是否让世界听到了另一种更震撼人心的音乐？因此，１９５５年５月１５日，当卡萨尔斯在全球音乐家的吁请下，在他流亡的法国南方小城普拉达"卡萨尔斯国际音乐节"上，重新演奏巴赫大提琴组曲。聆听他与音乐融为一体的发自肺腑的呻吟慨叹，人类怎能不为之颤栗？我十年前曾专程赴普拉达拜谒卡氏遗迹，小小的博物馆里，目睹他的圆眼镜、大提琴、石膏手模、用旧的旅行箱，特别是乐谱上细细研究每一小节的笔迹，我感到他、我父亲、我自己，哪有区别？古今中外艺术家的宿命精灵，哪有区别？这才是我们浑然如一的"家风"，如今，又叠加进布列顿和从他获得灵感的《叙事诗》，这全书三部，倘若真得神助，能穿透时空，抵达那些"鬼魂作曲家"云端的听觉，该多好。

我曾把不同类型的诗，戏分为"镇国之宝"和"玩艺儿"。简言之，当代中文诗，必在观念上大处着眼、技巧上小处着手。有大没小，则流于空疏；有小无大，则失之浅狭。"镇国之宝"，譬如青铜重器，须倾毕生举国之力熔铸而成，供奉神祖为其用，与馋嘴小儿口腹之欲无涉。证诸文学，《天问》、《离骚》、《史记》、《红楼》是也。虽太白璀璨、少陵沉郁、义山精雅、后主凄艳，不可比肩，盖因根本境界尚有不足。而当代中国，语言、现实、文化层层错位，每个有抱负的诗人，必须是思想者，除了"发出自己的天问"，别无他途。就是说，今天的中文诗，要么就是思想深刻到位的作品，要么就什么都不是。这儿，连成为"玩艺儿"的机会都没有，因为无论语言还是感觉，都是中外别人玩过的。我还有一命题，曰"作一个主动的他者"。是的，不仅有可见的外来"他者"，更有隐身的内在"他者"：我们一厢情愿以为能直线相连的中国古典，其实早已弃吾而去（更准确地说，被五四以来中国盛产的"文化虚无主义者"所摒弃）。我们的语言，在古汉语美学的字和外来概念的词之间分裂；我们的思维，在中、西生硬错位的语法关系间撕扯；我们的观念，常沦为一大堆摸不到感觉也不知其涵义的空洞词藻。二十世纪的中国，文化提问无比深刻，可我们据以应对那提问的，却是一片触目的空白！这厄运也并非中国独有，冷战之后、九一一之后，世界同样面临困惑：没有了不同社会理想之争，却更显出"大一统"的自私、玩世硬通货畅通无阻，"人"意义何在？"文学"意义何在？此刻每个人彻底孤独，举目四望，都在重重他者之间。这绝境正是唯一的真实。它很清楚地告诉我们，不要奢望可以轻易模拟、或复制任何现成的答案。我们唯一的出路，是破釜沉舟，变被动为主动，拉开审视的距离，由反思而自觉。自八十年代初，我们就谈论"人的自觉"和"诗的自觉"。如今，诗没离开提问者（天问者！）的位置，是世界转变成深深的自我怀疑，来印证诗思。我能感到，

"炼"出诗人真身。

我从来没为自己的诗作写过序或跋，原因之一是不希望助长读者的懒惰。他们应当从一行行诗句中读出诗人的苦心。但这次，我为《叙事诗》破了例，因为"家风"主题，既来自又超出此诗。《叙事诗》希冀传承的，乃是绵延三千余年的中文诗歌精美传统之风。因此，《叙事诗》的真正抱负，不能只停留在"为什么"写，它必须落实为"如何写"这个作品上？用我阅读别人作品的尺度，就是第一看完整的人生经验，第二看提炼思想的能力，而最终看如何呈现为作品。我给这部长诗定的标准，一言以蔽之，是极端"形式主义的"。全书的整体音乐构思、三部分之间的节奏对比、每部标题中点明的时间意识、每部专门设计的结构、每首诗独特的韵律（包括刻意的无韵体）、以及不同意象的活力等等，基于诗意的深化推进，而"持续地赋予形式"。形式就是思想。当代中文诗必须抛弃粗劣而重获精雅，植根个人又与古典神似。我希望，通过这部独创的作品，能一圆折磨新诗近一百年的"新古典"之梦。同时，也请读者注意，这些诗句间"家风"劲吹。第一部"照相册"，从我诞生第一天的照片始，到我母亲剪贴完照相册、次日清晨猝然去世止，把一个回顾中几乎非现实的童年，用一个个日期牢牢锁定。第二部"水薄荷哀歌"，用五首哀歌，梳理贯穿我个人沧桑的五大主题：现实、爱情、历史、故乡、诗歌，直到时间幻象被剥去，人类不变的处境展示无遗。第三部"哲人之墟"，那"墟"在哪里？除了我们耽于深思的内心，它能在哪里？历史无所谓悲喜，它仅仅归结于此。"两次来到／洗劫后的洁净　月光的幽咽／缕缕幽香让你听你在逍遥"。没错，倘若你嗅觉灵敏，这风就有老庄味儿，有佛祖味儿，有苏格拉底味儿，它掠过无数"思想面具"，粼粼拂动我手中"月色和这首诗两个表面"，把一个人的"空书"，变成"火中满溢之书"。

《叙事诗》这样的极端之作，当然被一般出版者视为剧毒。

但台北联经出版公司，愿意出版它，且倾全力精美出版之，令我刮目相看之余，更为感动。在全球商业化的恶俗中，仍有秉持古雅中文诗歌"家风"者。由是，诗人的书桌上盘旋而起的清新之气，方绵延不绝。我想，正因为这个贯穿了古今中外诗人的血缘，让我不仅是幸存者，更堪称幸运者。***

树欲静而不能静，该抱怨自己定力不够。而家风不可止。我信，它永不休止。

杨炼
２０１０年１０月１１日伦敦改定
Revised 21.8.2015

* 《洪荒时代——赠张枣》，见杨炼诗集《李河谷的诗》。
***
《叙事诗》这样的极端之作，当然被一般出版者视为剧毒。但Bloodaxe Books，愿意出版它，且倾全力精美出版之，令我刮目相看之余，更为感动。在全球商业化的恶俗中，仍有秉持古雅诗歌"家风"者。由是，诗人的书桌上盘旋而起的清新之气，方绵延不绝。我想，正因为这个贯穿了古今中外诗人的血缘，让我不仅是幸存者，更堪称幸运者。

PREFACE

Family Tradition

Zhang Zao passed away in March 2010, and the early death of this talented poet had us all wringing our hands in distress: he was the first of our generation to die through illness, rather than accidentally or violently.[1] His death had nothing dramatic about it, unlike those of Haizi[2] or Gu Cheng,[3] yet it did point up how immensely impermanent life is. I have no intention of adding to the chorus of elegies for Zhang Zao, because, in the early spring of 2001, I wrote a small one for him (and for myself too, of course). The poem is called *Chaotic Era*:[4] it was written after we had met by chance in Paris and gone strolling all night through the beautiful silent streets, chatting to our hearts' content about family and about poetry until morning, when we got on our different trains and went our separate ways. There is a prophecy in the poem:

write well   then write up to the revenge of a gloomy life

And there is also no lack of approval, such as this line:

a family tradition of white cranes

I particularly like that last one. Family Tradition[5] – oh, how long I've been parted from that! I enjoy this typical Chinese combination of words: its two parts are entirely independent images with no

---

1. Zhang Zao 张枣 (1962-2010) died from cancer.

2. Hai Zi 海子 was the pen name of poet Zha Haisheng 查海生 (1964-1989), who committed suicide on a railway line in March 1989.

3. Gu Cheng 顾城 (1956-1993) poet and essayist: In October 1993 in New Zealand, Gu Cheng killed his wife with an axe before hanging himself.

4. See Yang Lian, *Lee Valley Poems* (Tarset: Bloodaxe Books, 2009), p.95, tr. Brian Holton and Agnes Hung-Chong Chan. Lightly modified from the original publication.

5. The Chinese term is 家风: i.e. *jia* home/family + *feng* wind; custom/ usage. In this Preface there are recurring puns on the double senses of *feng*.

obligatory link between them, but they combine into a seamless garment to make space for the imagination. What kind of tradition is worthy of blowing from the public entrance hall to intimacy of the family's inner rooms? On reflection, is there something more there, apart from the tradition of individual moral virtue? Ah, but this tradition wasn't passed down in my family, for it was my family that was actually passed down by the tradition! So the rising breeze has nothing to do with the drifting duckweed of Song Yu's *Rhapsody on the Wind*,[6] but is a tradition that rises in our blood and travels far through the knowledge that is handed down through a family, that arrives to buffet and to blast, that stretches into the far distance to touch us now. Its profile is visible firstly in our attitude to how we conduct ourselves in society, and secondly in matters of propriety and good taste. What is called nobility and elegance (arrogance, even) has nothing to do with literary ornament, but ultimately relies on a vigorous and characterful spirit with an ancient origin. From the opening line of *On Encountering Trouble*,[7]

> *Scion of the high lord Gao Yang,*

Qu Yuan went on to speak of his *inward beauty*, which is perfectly consonant with this. Even though the *family tradition of white cranes* was maligned and trashed again and again in the turbulence that racked 20th-century Mainland China, I do believe that an intangible *family tradition of white cranes* endures in the minds of solitary individuals, and if that tradition were to be broken we could still recover it, so long as there are people alive, just as we could rediscover the entire aesthetic tradition of Chinese poetry from the intrinsic character of the Chinese writing system itself.

---

6. Song Yu 宋玉 (*c*. 319-298 BC). Poet, to whom some of the verses in *Songs of the South* were traditionally ascribed, as well as some early poems in the *fu* 賦 genre, including *Feng fu* 风赋 (*Wind Fu*).

7. See David Hawkes, tr. (1985, etc.), *The Songs of the South* (Harmondsworth: Penguin Books), p.68. Qu Yuan 屈原, the putative author, is held to have lived from the 4th to the 3rd century BC, and is the first named poet in the history of China. The long poem *Heavenly Questions* attributed to him is referred to below.

Zhang Zao was quite excited when he got to read my poem, and he said, 'I'll write a good poem in response to yours, for sure!' Only after he was gone did I hear about his *Crane Poems*, which he wrote just before he died so prematurely: is there some connection there? I don't know. But I can be certain that a blast of Family Tradition had blown his way.

If I wantonly speak of Family Tradition by way of a preface to *Narrative Poem*, I may be suspected of wandering off-topic. Some over-serious readers may also ask if this isn't just a recycling of Yu Luoke's *On Descent*?[8] I must therefore explain clearly that, while Family Tradition is indeed linked to rank and station in society, rank and station are not the same thing as class, especially not the 'Class Theory' inculcated in us for so long and which we accepted so naïvely and uncomprehendingly, or the 'Class Struggle' which shackled us inside a new caste system and which we were compelled on pain of death to join. Within the context of traditional gentry society in China, it might be said that Family Tradition was founded on property, but it would be much better to say that its origins lie in education and training that ran progressively deeper with each passing generation, so it has an instinctive distrust of the nouveau riche, preferring to set figures like Tao Yuanming[9] or Cao Xueqin[10] as standards of value and worth – now, tell me, what class did they belong to, these geniuses who died in poverty? Why should someone who is a failure in financial terms not have a first-class mind?

---

8. Yu Luoke 遇罗克 (1942-1970) was executed after being accused of contradicting Communist Party dogma by arguing that social class might not necessarily be inherited.

9. Tao Yuanming 陶渊明 (AD 365-427), first and perhaps greatest of the Recluse Poets, he famously resigned from government service to live a simple life in rural retirement.

10. Cao Xueqin 曹雪芹 (1715 or 1724-1763 or 1764), author of a great masterpiece, the long novel *The Story of the Stone*. Son of a once rich and influential family who fell from Imperial grace, he died poor, in the western suburbs of Beijing. See Cao Xueqin, tr. David Hawkes & John Minford (1973 etc.), *The Story of the Stone*, 5 vols. (Harmondsworth: Penguin Books).

In *Narrative Poem*, which is permeated with autobiographical elements, my father plays an important role. The story of his early years is that he was born into a wealthy family whose property included the Fortune Theatre,[11] but, though at first an enthusiast for Kunqu Opera,[12] he became very attached to Western classical music, and by the time he graduated from university, he had an extensive knowledge of it. His six years as a diplomat in Switzerland after 1949, served, along with the European way of life, to convince him even more of the rational beauty which infuses music. But when the Cultural Revolution began in 1966, and Beethoven was roundly criticised as 'representative of capitalist culture', my father faced a painful choice: as a CCP member, he should trust the party absolutely, yet as an individual, he clearly felt that the music was filled with love and beauty. So which command was he to obey? This problem, now so elementary that it is no longer an issue, was unimaginably grave at that time. If he declared for his own feelings, then how could he not be judged as having betrayed his family, having betrayed the road he'd struggled towards for half his life, and having betrayed the bright future that China was promised? It was hard, but in the end, he was my father, and finally he chose beauty, though his heart was breaking. He maintained that beauty was not wrong, though betrayal was. It was only long after I heard this story that I understood: was it because of this that, even while the storm was gathering ominously outside our window, our family was able to preserve a little micro-climate of reason and love, which allowed me to grow up relatively sound and psychologically whole? What I admire is not that he identified with Beethoven, but that this identification itself embodied a kind of strength that emanated from humanity, and the strength to re-examine history. So I wrote those lines in *Hometown Elegy* with compete conviction:

---

11. One of the most famous Peking Opera theatres, it was established in 1906 in Goldfish Lane, next to Dong'an Market, Beijing. It was demolished in 1993.

12. Pronounced *kwunCHOO*. See http://www.unesco.org/culture/ich/index.php?lg=en&pg=00011&RL=00004 (accessed 13 September 2015).

> *bypass the starry firmament   slow steps towards father*
> *return to the origin of the allegory of self*

Narrative Poem was written over a period of more than four years, between 2005 and 2009. It is the most comprehensive expression so far of my thinking and my poetics. In a sense, it turns all my previous work into a first draft, into a single stage of my progress. What I mean by this is the progression from the 'China Manuscript' stage summed up by *Yi*[13] through the 'South Pacific Manuscript' style represented by my poem cycle *Where the Sea Stands Still*[14] to the 'Europe Manuscript' beginning with the long poem *Concentric Circles*[15] and also including the independent collections which appeared between these major works, which I have termed the 'Thought-Art Project'. The difficulty of *Narrative Poem*, in comparison with previous work, lies with its concrete, specific, and original poetry, which must necessarily stand up to the scrutiny of universal experience and common history. To narrate the events in the life of one person in one family, as touching and living through a '*point of destiny*', is to encompass all of 20th-century China's complex and cataclysmic changes – in reality, in culture and even in literature. To sum it up in two questions, how does history become entangled with individual destiny? How does an individual's inner being form historical depth? As each of us is a metaphor for history, the *Narrative* of an essentially human quandary is what this *Poem* points to. The title *Narrative Poem* is thus completely directed towards thought. Its structure is lightly infused with an inheritance from the Family Tradition: as I was envisioning *Narrative Poem*, I happened to hear three cello suites by the 20th-century English composer Benjamin Britten, and their rambling depth and serenity were deeply

---

13. Yang Lian, tr. Mabel Lee, *Yi* (Copenhagen, Los Angeles: Green Integer, 2002).

14. Yang Lian, tr. Brian Holton, *Where the Sea Stands Still: New Poems* (Newcastle upon Tyne: Bloodaxe Books, 1999).

15. Yang Lian, tr. Brian Holton & Agnes Hung-Chong Chan, *Concentric Circles* (Tarset: Bloodaxe Books, 2005).

moving; though their tone is modern, in their detail they can be traced directly back to J.S. Bach's six famous suites for solo cello. I only learned much later that Britten's piece was actually written in response to Bach's cello suites. The 20th century's greatest cellist, Pablo Casals, had apparently rehearsed the six Bach suites for all of twelve years, and then one day, as he played them, what had been withered and dried-up was transfigured, and the faded antique colours began to reveal unfathomable depths, and not only lovable ones, either. Quite the opposite, for they can be terrifying too. From the fifties onwards, my father has absolutely adored Casals' playing, and especially the six Bach cello suites. Maybe my father just didn't know about the heroism of the man: from 1937 to 1955, in protest at the dictatorship of General Franco, Casals refused to perform at events in any Nazi state, any dictatorship or any state whose 'standpoint was unclear'. That is, he was silent in those parts of the world for eighteen years. Would the deepest silence let the world hear new music that would stun the human heart? On 15th May 1955, in response to the pleas of musicians all over the world, Casals played the Bach cello suites again at the Pablo Casals Festival in the little southern French town of Prades. Those who listened to player and music melting into one let out deep and heartfelt groans, for how could humans not hear this and tremble? Ten years ago, I made a special journey to Prades, to pay my respects to Casals' remains, and in the little museum there I saw his spectacles, his cello, plaster casts of his hands, his battered suitcase, and, in particular, I saw his tiny annotations to the score, whose every bar he had investigated in detail, and I felt there was no real difference between him, my father and myself. Is there any difference between the fated spirit of artists, whether ancient or modern, Chinese or non-Chinese? That is the real Family Tradition, within which we are all absolutely the same, and how wonderful it would be now, if *Narrative Poem*, layering Benjamin Britten and the inspiration I took from him, if this whole three-part book really had ancestral help, if it were able to pass through space and time to reach high above the clouds, and into the hearing of those *Ghost Composers*.

I once jokingly divided different types of poetry into National Treasures and Playthings. Simply put, contemporary Chinese poetry must take the long view in terms of its concepts, as well as handle the detail in terms of its technique. If there is the former but not the latter, it will decline into empty verbiage, and if the reverse, it will fail through narrow superficiality. National Treasures such as our ancient ritual bronzes, whose casting must have consumed the entire nation's energies over a lifetime, and whose function was to make offerings to the holy ancestors, had nothing to do with the desire of greedy children for sustenance. So it is too in literature, with Qu Yuan's *Heavenly Questions*,[16] Sima Qian's *Historical Records*,[17] and Cao Queqin's *The Story of the Stone*.[18] Though Li Bai is dazzling, Du Fu melancholy,[19] Li Shangyin[20] elegant and sophisticated, and Li Yu[21] gorgeously rancorous, they cannot stand beside the three masterworks cited, because none of them attained such heights of the human spirit. In contemporary China, language, reality and culture are all dislocated on many levels, and anyone who has ambitions to be a poet must also be a thinker, for apart from proposing their own *Heavenly Questions* there is no other route for them. That is to say, today's Chinese poetry is either up to standard in its thinking, or it is nothing. There seems no point in linking back to the Playthings here, because everything, whether language or feeling, has been played with before, in China and elsewhere. And

---

16. See note 7 above.

17. Sima Qian 司马迁 (*d.* 86 BC), the father of Chinese historiography. His Historical Records 《史记》 was the model for all of the official dynastic histories which followed it. See Burton Watson, *Ssu-ma Ch'ien: Grand Historian of China* (New York: Columbia University Press, 1958).

18. See note 10 above.

19. Li Bai 李白 (701–762) and his younger friend Du Fu 杜甫 (712–770) have long been acclaimed as the two greatest poets of the golden age of classical poetry in China.

20. Li Shangyin 李商隐 (*c.* 813–858), one of the great poets of the Late Tang period: his poetry is dense, allusive, very difficult, and very beautiful.

21. Li Yu 李煜 (*c.* 937–978) last emperor of the Southern Tang dynasty, and the first master of the lyric form (*ci* 词).

I have another proposition: Be The Active Other. Yes, not only the external and visible Other, but also the hidden internal Other: in our fantasies we imagine there can be a straight-line connection from the classics to us, but in fact, that connection has long been lost (or, more accurately, it was discarded and abandoned by the Cultural Nihilists that China has been producing in the hundred years since the May Fourth Movement).[22] Our language is split between characters derived from the aesthetics of archaic Chinese and words derived from non-Chinese concepts; our thinking is torn apart by synaptic connections derived from the harsh dislocation of east from west; our ideas are too often reduced to a mass of inexplicable feelings and empty rhetoric of no discernible meaning. Cultural questions were incomparably weighty for China in the 20th century, but when we looked for answers to these questions, we found only a perfect and evident blank! This unhappy state is not at all unique to China, for after the Cold War and 9/11 the world now faces the same puzzle: if there is no struggle between differing social ideals, but only an ever-more manifest Union of Selfishness and Cynicism in the charade that is the unimpeded circulation of hard cash, then what is the significance of the individual? What is the significance of literature? At this moment every individual is utterly isolated and alone, surrounded wherever he or she looks by ring upon ring of Others. This impasse is our one and only reality. It tells us very clearly that we cannot realistically expect to be able to simulate or duplicate any superficial ready-made response. Our only escape is to take an axe to the sinking ship, turn reaction into action, open up a space for close scrutiny, and through self-reflection become aware. Since the early eighties of last century, we have been talking about 'human awareness' and 'poetic awareness'. Now, it is not poetry that has abandoned the position of being a questioner (a *Heavenly* one!), but the world which has changed to admit a deep self-doubt, thus confirming the insights of the poets. I can feel a

---

22. This refers to the movement of 1915–1921, which is also called the New Culture Movement.

crisis in human thought more acute than the economic crisis, a longing for poetic masterworks. This, this is the moment to forge a National Treasure. This, precisely this, is the vital inspiration for contemporary Chinese poetry.

Narrative Poem is a long poem. There is a hidden connection between it and my other two long poems, *Yi* and *Concentric Circles*, in that they form a dialectic of Thesis, Antithesis, and Synthesis, or, precisely, China, Non-China, and the Unity of China and Non-China. *Yi* has its roots in the symbol system of the *Book of Change*,[23] opened up to the experience of contemporary China, and is a realisation of a large-scale language experiment using seven different kinds of poem and three different kinds of prose. The poem and the poet himself

can only then be truly born in death's shape.

The concrete details in *Concentric Circles* come from the experience of exile in different places, and it spans both Chinese and non-Chinese cultures, using an all-pervasive spatial awareness to organise itself into five overlapping circles, layer upon layer (or deepening circles, layer beneath layer?), and that structure, while it might be said to be a poetic one, might be better described as philosophical, as it turns time into space, placing one's self as a questioner at the centre of the universe, and its ideological concentric circles finally replace a linear theory of evolution and a formation of a mode of thought that is

moved once again by an ancient betrayal.

The unique context in which contemporary China finds itself out of necessity compels our work to combine two characteristics: the conceptual and the experimental. Even if we only write a single line of poetry, we have to combine all our resources, ancient and modern, Chinese and non-Chinese. Lacking this ocean of potential, the lines that float over the white paper will not qualify to be called

---

23. See John Minford, tr. *I Ching* (New York: Viking, 2014).

a poem. For the same reason, it is not only length that is implied by a long poem. Long must be identical with *deep*, and we have to make it *new* for a depth never before expressed. So, when I read a long poem, I hope, in the first place, to see the writer realise the totality of his or her life experience, and, next, to see the power of the philosophical thought abstracted from that experience, with the final stage only then being the assessment of the degree of the work's completion, and its success or failure as a whole. I have to acknowledge that, here, *deep* means *difficult*. In today's China, so addicted to instant results and fast returns, poets are either mired in a geriatric adolescence that interminably repeats their youthful emissions, or are doing perfunctory and slipshod work that displays the startling contrast between wholesale quantity and barren infertility in their poems. It's not in fact very hard to play at being avant-garde, but it is very hard to become an *arrière-garde* with a different phase of writing as its after-effect. Poetry is the best-ever footnote to the injunction *festina lente*.[24] It took me five years to write *Yi*, four years for *Concentric Circles*, and now, more than four years for *Narrative Poem*. More than thirteen years of my heart's blood, for these three long poems, a meticulous slowness, and it is only with hindsight that the speed of it is visible, for, to my surprise, it was over very quickly. To go back to my father's maxims for life, in all things you should first 'Find pleasure in what you do' and second, 'Take it slow'. And these two sayings are, you may say, the highest expression of the art of writing. To write is to seek enlightenment, to cultivate the self, and it is not the poet who makes the poetry, but the poetry which makes the poet. The slow fire of poetry, cloistered and shy, forges and refines the poet himself.[25]

I have never before written a preface or an afterword to my poetry, and the reason for this is that I hoped not to aid and abet idleness in my readers. Readers should puzzle out, line by line, the pains

---

24. Latin proverb: *make haste slowly*.
25. There is a pun here on Yang Lian's personal name: *lian* 炼 can be glossed as *smelt, refine, temper*.

the poet has taken with the poems. But this time I have made an exception, because the topic of Family Tradition both comes out of and goes beyond the bounds of this poem. *Narrative Poem* aspires to become part of the tradition, being in the style of the refined poetic tradition of China, which has persisted unbroken for over three thousand years. The real ambition of *Narrative Poem*, then, can it simply end with the why of writing, or must it not put into effect within the work itself the how of writing? The yardstick I use when reading other people's writing is, as I said, to first look for how the writer realises the totality of his or her life experience, and, next, to see the power of the philosophical thought abstracted from that experience, then, lastly, see how the work presents itself. The standard I set for these long poems was, in a word, extreme Formalism. The overall musical structure of the book as a whole, the rhythmic contrasts between its three chapters, the time-awareness indicated in the headings, all the expressly devised structures, the unique metrics of each component poem (including the deliberate use of blank verse), the vitality of the different images, and so on, these were all used with the aim of advancing a deepened poetics and a sustained contribution to Form. Form is thought. Contemporary Chinese poetry must cast aside the cheap and the shoddy in order to recover its elegance again and take root in the affinity between the individual and the classical. I hope to be able, by means of this original work, to grind down with one turn of the wheel New Verse's near-century-old dream of a New Classicism. At the same time, and I ask the reader to note this, a gale of Family Tradition is howling through these lines of poetry. The first section, *Photograph Album*, beginning from a photograph taken on the day I was born, goes up to the day my mother finished pasting the photographs into the album before dying suddenly and unexpectedly the following morning, and it firmly fixes each date by looking back at a near-unreal childhood. In the second section, *Watermint Elegy*, five elegies tease out five major themes that run through the cataclysmic changes in my life, viz. reality, love, history, home, and poetry, until the illusion of time is stripped away, and the unchanging human quandary is comprehensively laid bare. In the third part, *Ruin*

29

of a Sage, where are the ruins? Where could they be, except in our inner hearts, lost in deep meditation? History has no so-called joys and sorrows, for in the end it all comes down to no more than this:

twice arrived-at
post-looted cleanness   moonlight's whimper
wafts of faint perfume   let you hear you are free as the air.

That's right: if your sense of smell is acute enough, you will detect a waft of Laozi and Zhuangzi, something of the Buddhist patriarchs, a touch of Socrates, all sweeping by innumerable Thinking Masks, brushing with crystalline clarity against the *surfaces of moonlight* and this poem, turning one person's *Empty Book* into a *Book Brimming with Fire*.

A work of extremes like *Narrative Poem* is, of course, anathema to normal publishers. Yet Bloodaxe Books have been willing to publish it, and have done all they can to make a fine book of it, which moves me, and leaves me with an increased respect for them. In the commercialised global vulgarity that surrounds us, there are still some who hold out for the Family Tradition of refined classical elegance in poetry. So the pure breezes that blow over a poet's desk are uninterrupted still. It seems to me that it is precisely this consanguinity linking poets ancient and modern, Chinese and non-Chinese, that allows me not only to be a survivor, but also, you may say, to be one of the lucky ones.

Trees that desire silence but cannot be silent will murmur at their lack of *Sāmadhībala*, the meditator's gentle strength of will. At the same time, the winds of Family Tradition will not cease to blow. I believe they never will.

YANG LIAN
11th October 2011, London
Revised September 2015, Berlin

第一部

照像册：有时间的梦

（不太快的快板）

PART 1

PHOTOGRAPH ALBUM: DREAM OF TIME

(*Allegro ma non troppo*)

照像册之一：

1955. 2.22——1955. 5. 4.

瑞士，伯尔尼。

PHOTOGRAPH ALBUM 1

22nd February 1955 – 4th May 1955

Berne, Switzerland

诗章之一：鬼魂作曲家

这看不见的　鬼魂写下的结构
搭建一座红色演奏厅
子宫中小嘴抿着鲜红的淤泥
蛆虫似的五指　拱出就抓着母亲
抓紧一页热烘烘的乐谱
珍珠白的粘液涂满一把大提琴
猛地拉响　胎儿都挂在音符上

　　　　　　　聆听　起点上沉溺的结构

胎儿就是音符　一粒腥香的珠子
没分裂出四肢已被钉牢了
刚在卵里动　已摇碎一片铃声了
乐曲吐出浸透蔚蓝油彩的枝头

闭上眼听鸟鸣串成虚线
绿叶　用舌尖舔进一条弓弦的老
拈着鬼魂储存的皱纹花
一把大提琴像枚干贝壳呼应大海的浩瀚
一次倒空一千次倒叙中的呜咽
闭上眼　精液化开黑暗
　　　　　　　网尽银亮亮的鱼群

小耳朵里肉还在流　流入一种思想
小鬼魂忘情哼唱　世界忘情逗留
在血红的元素里

这是五月　风中满是啼哭
一把老教堂祭坛前空荡荡的木椅子
回顾着　等着他到来

Canto 1: Ghost Composer

this unseen structure   written by a ghost
sets up a red auditorium
the little mouth in the womb sipping at scarlet sludge
maggot-like fingers   arching to grab at mother
grabbing red-hot sheet music
the cello spattered with pearl-white mucus
has been abruptly bowed   the foetus hangs on that notation

listen   to the submerged structure at its inception

the foetus is the notation   a pearl of rancid perfume
its still undifferentiated limbs already nailed down
a moment ago squirming in the egg   it has shaken apart the bell's ring
the music spews branches saturated with sky-blue greasepaint

close your eyes and hear birdsong string up a dotted line
green leaves   tongues licking into the dotage of a bowstring
twisting wrinkled flowers stockpiled by ghosts
like a dried scallop the cello echoes the ocean's vast enormity
pouring out emptiness once pouring out sobs a thousand times in flashback
close your eyes   semen dissolves the darkness
a silvery-bright shoal in the net's tail

flesh still flowing in the little ears   flowing into a sort of thought
a little ghost calm in wordless song   a world calm in loitering
inside an element of blood red

this is May   the wind is full of weeping
a wooden chair quite empty by the classroom altar
turns around   waiting for him to arrive

"第一天"

山上的雪　溶解在阳光里
也刚刚滑出一条隧道
这小兽　侧着睡

一场哭过的风暴
填满枕头上香喷喷的凹陷
嫩如菌丝的黑发咸而潮

缩进白线套的指爪　微微颤
一场海啸托起水手的小床
又一个人质抵押给家园

山上的雪　平行于桅杆上的眺望
他加入厌倦的无尽的人形
返回　意味着亲吻下一道波浪

一张照片停住窗外针叶林的青葱
黎明按下快门的一刹那
他爱上自己不在的梦中梦

被软的礁石撞碎　而抵达
黑的无知　白的无知
苦的松香　记得树干上狠狠地摩擦

'First day'

snow on the mountains   melting in sunlight
and just slipped out of a tunnel too
this little beast   sleeps on its side

a weeping frenzy
fills in the hollows on the bolster
mycelium-fine hair damp and briny

paws shrunk into a coverlet of white mittens   tremble faintly
a tsunami picks up the sailor's little cot
another hostage mortgaged to home and family

snow on the mountains   parallel to the masthead watchers
he is added to endless weary human forms
returning   implies kissing the next ocean breakers

beyond the windowpane a photo stops the pine wood's green
the instant daybreak hits the shutter
he falls in love with the dream in the dream that he isn't here

shattered on a soft reef   to have reached
ignorance of black   ignorance of white
bitter rosin   fierce friction on tree-trunks remembered

"第十天"

市场上扑面砸来的雪亮　太熟悉
当车门的自动锁卡嗒轻响
他的眼睛三十年后依然紧闭

寒意把生命磨快　这束光
金黄　奶味儿　远离象征
被护士的手拢在床边上

海豹的小鼻孔筲在被单的海浪中
天竺葵和柠檬　三十年后答案妖艳
当初却是疑问　用缝合眼皮的疼

把第十天的世界缝在外面
第十次扣着扳机的光已是谚语
他被射中　追赶一道来复线

至死延长的　自天空雪崩的性质
枕着雪水思维的双脚
隶属一个金黄奶味儿的地理

叠印在心里　跨出车门就踩到
果肉突然惊醒的酸涩的颗粒
他以光速隐在瞎了的鹅卵石间闪耀

'Tenth day'

in the market snow's brightness slaps your face   too well-known
as the car's automatic door lock snicks softly shut
his eyes are still firmly closed thirty years on

the keen chill whets life   the sheaves of light
golden   milky-tasting   far from symbolic
by a nurse's hand at the bedside held tight

the seal's little nostrils rise from the whitecap coverlet
geranium and lemon   a seductive solution thirty years on
though there's doubt then   with sewn-up eyelids' hurt

sewing the tenth-day world onto what's external
light's tenth pull on the trigger already an axiom
he's shot   chasing the rifling of the barrel

whose nature lengthens unto death   avalanche sky-fallen
both feet pillowed on melt-water's line of thought
at the command of a geography milky-tasting and golden

double exposure in the mind   leaps the car door and lands on
suddenly-wakened acrid pellets of fruit-flesh
hidden by light-speed among blind cobbles he blazes on

母亲的手迹

她的手抚摸　死后还抚摸
深海里一枝枝白珊瑚
被层层动荡的蓝折射

冷如精选的字　给儿子写第一封家书
亲笔的　声声耳语中海水冲刷
海流翻阅一张小脸的插图

跟随笔划　一页页长大
一滴血被称为爱　从开端起
就稔熟每天粘稠一点的语法

儿子的回信只能逆着时间投递
儿子的目光修改阅读的方向
读到　一场病抖着捧不住一个字

她的手断了　她的海悬在纸上
隔开一寸远　墨迹的蓝更耀眼
体温凝进这个没有风能翻动的地方

珊瑚灯　衬着血丝编织的傍晚
淡淡照出一首诗分娩的时刻
当所有语言响应一句梗在心里的遗言

Mother's handwriting

her hand gently strokes   after death still stroking
each white deep-sea coral branch
refracted through layer on layer of blue roiling

cold as carefully-chosen words   the first letter written to her son
in her own hand   the seawater scours with its murmuring
through images of a little face currents are glancing

with her scribbles   page by page growing
a drop of blood called love   from the start
each day into stickier grammar ripening

only against the tide of time can the son's reply be delivered
the son's gaze changes the direction of reading
reads up to   an illness when he can't hold a word for shivering

her cut-off hands   above the page her ocean hanging
a single inch away   the blue ink still more dazzling
body heat curdles into a place the wind can't blow down

coral lamp   sets off a twilight blood-plaited
faintly lighting the moment of a poem in childbirth
as all language responds to dying words in a heart obstructed

"满月"

第一个月的圆圆杯口里还将掬进
多少个月　　那孩子才静静躺在水底
成为远眺的清晨的一部分

早醒了　　小小的蛙类或剑鱼
张着五指间的蹼　　眼珠闪闪游向
窗口　　水族馆明媚恐怖的玻璃

第一个月的云　　腹部有鳞熠熠发亮
第一个春天俯身痒痒亲着他的脸
鸟鸣用彩绘的尾巴拖着小床

还不知有个过去呢　　不知血腥的循环
弹奏在睫毛上　　没有人的黎明
每个细胞都是艘偏离航线的船

交给一次触礁的激情
那孩子的乖　　耗尽了未来的缄默
拨着秒针的阳光亮度中

已懂得最深的哭不必说
襁褓盛着一个月长大一岁的小海豚
眼里满含惊异　　轻轻溅落进漩涡

42

'First month fulfilled'

into the round lip of the First Moon's cup will pour
so many moons   now the child lies quiet underwater
turns into part of the dawning seen from afar

little frog or swordfish   early waking
opens the webs between its five fingers   gleaming pupils wandering
to a window   a fish tank's bright beautiful glass

First Month clouds   belly fish-scales brightly shimmer
the first Spring bends down to give his cheek a scratchy kiss
a colourful tail of birdsong dragging the little cot over

still doesn't know the past exists   doesn't know the bloody circulation
plucking at his eyelashes   non-person's daybreak
each cell a boat wandered from its true navigation

delivering the once-only passion of being dashed on a rocky strand
this child's good behaviour   has exhausted the future's reticence
uproots the sunshine brilliance of the clock's second hand

he has understood the deepest of tears must not be spoken
little dolphin in swaddling clothes, one year old in a day
eyes full of amazement   gently splashing into the maelstrom

"五十天"

大海像母亲滞留于别处的身体
她仅剩的一双手　切除到照片上
睡衣的波纹一条蓝一条绿

袖子高高挽着　温润的光
抱起他　满溢香皂味儿的海岸
告诉他毕生得枕着海风的臂膀

毕生湿淋淋从洗澡盆向上看
小小的裸体攀登一条被包扎的脐带
小小的茎　用水声的易逝的方言

和母亲继续交谈　她的不在
剪断了　漂白了　注射进儿子时
明艳如鸥迹无所不在

甚至大海也会死　就像词
死了　才捞起他　皮肤贴着梦游
一只洗澡盆中一场迷失练习

拉住一双嵌进小小腋窝的手
换成大海的也被认出　儿子体重里
躺入母亲的碎　他　忍住这享受

'Fifty days'

the ocean is like mother's body detained elsewhere
the only hands she has left   cut off in the photo
rippling stripes of blue and green on her nightwear

sleeves rolled all the way up   a mild and kindly embrace
of light enfolds him   a seashore overflowing with the scent of soap
telling him he'll lay his head on the sea breeze's shoulder all his days

looking up sopping wet from the bathtub all his days
at tiny nakedness climbing a parcelled-up umbilicus
a tiny stalk   with the fleeting patois the water says

chatting with mother   her non-existence
cut off   bleached   when injected into her son
brightly beautiful as the ubiquitous seagull footprints

even the sea will die too   just like words may
have died   then scoop him up   skin sticky with his dream journey
a lesson in the bathtub on going astray

pulling at a hand embedded in a tiny armpit
it is also known that hand becomes ocean   in a son's body weight
lying down in mother's fragments   he   endures this delight

"七十天——五月四日"

野鸭子揣着一根宝石蓝的羽毛
在他雪白衣襟的小湖里游
弯成两个时刻的眼眉　　泼出笑

候鸟被一块植入头脑的磁石引诱
飞啊　　两个日期间的意义
烫伤一双手　　令字体更娟秀

发育成小广场上水灵灵的鹅卵石
颠着婴儿车　　和俯身好奇的太阳
雪山像一支烟袅袅燃起

诀别水灵灵的　　竹林托着的雨香
洇开万里外　　他倒影的水声幽闭症
第一天已铸成挣扎不出的疯狂

野鸭的翡翠脖子在背上滚动
一根海岸的轴旋拧三百六十度
他缝合的玩具童年　　只留下针孔

他赝品似的今天　　云的软体动物
缕缕爬过山脊　　活着的征兆
嘎　　嘎　　野鸭橘红的舌尖正在表述

'Seventy days – May 4th'

a wild duck with a lapis lazuli feather tucked in its shoulder
voyages on the little lake of his snow-white lapel
bent into momentary eyebrows   spilling out laughter

migrant birds are seduced by a brain-implanted magnet
oh flight!   the meaning that lies between two dates
burns both hands   makes the shape of the script more delicate

grown into a cobblestone in the little square and wide awake
jolting the pram   and the curious sun leaning over it
snowy mountains like curling cigarette smoke

farewell to wide awake   bamboo draws out the rain's perfume
blotting out a million miles   the water's sound he reflects is stifling
first day already forged into a madness there's no struggling from

lolling on its back the duck's neck all bright greens
a seashore axis twisted through 360 degrees
of the soft toys of his childhood   only the needle's eye remains

this today of his is like a fake   mollusc clouds
have endlessly climbed the ridge   portents of living
quack   quack   duck's orange tongue still explaining

照相册之二：

1955. 7.23——1974.4

中国，北京。

PHOTOGRAPH ALBUM 2

23rd July 1955 – April 1974

Beijing, China

诗章之二：鬼魂作曲家

　　　　　　这逐一递增的阴影的结构
逐一消失　　当照像册移向一个傍晚

　　　　　　这大提琴兀自鸣响
应和鬼魂持续的　　低音的沉思

黄昏的光组成纹丝不动的音节
抚摸静听的脸　　镶进一张张旧照的
回旋加深的暮色　　准备好给一夜收藏的
紫丁香　　细数芳香的时间

奔跑的孩子限定他笔直冲入的每一天

这页乐谱上　　睡眠呢喃归来
轻吻印在眼皮上也像一种演奏
走过肉里花簇粉红的林荫道也是演奏
整个留在别处的春天　　被照片夹满书签
忘了对谁发出微笑　　远远问谁在笑

这页乐谱上　　回声翻阅着
　　　　　　　　一个把大海变没的结构

消失进酷似一扇玫瑰窗的天空里去
鬼魂的倾诉以孩子为刻度
想像粉碎寂静的　　推着海底的岩石
想像被寂静粉碎的　　撕碎丝质的蝴蝶
平铺纸页间一轮绚丽的落月
想像　　饱蘸灰烬的笔尖沙沙书写
一场风暴逼入历史的休止符
琴弓拉过　　光迸溅

递增没有的现在那无始无终的现在
粉碎之后的寂静

Canto 2: Ghost Composer

                one by one these shadow structures grow by degrees
disappear one by one   as the photo album moves toward evening

                these cellos still sounding
should be the soul's *sostenuto*   a bass meditation

gloaming light is composed on a motionless mode
stroking the silently listening face   mounting photos one by one
circling a deeper dusk   prepared from lilacs collected
all night long   the time of perfumed countdown

a rushing child confines his bolt upright dash into each day

on this page of the score   muttering sleep-talk returns
gentle kisses imprinted on eyelids seem a sort of performance too
walking across an avenue of pink bouquets is a performance too
a whole springtime left elsewhere   pressed full of bookmarks by photos
forgetting who the smile was for   asking from far off who was smiling

on this page of the score   echoes glance through
                a structure that makes the ocean cease to exist

disappearing into a sky terribly like a rose window
the ghost's outpouring takes children for its gauge
imagining rocks that shatter silence   that shove the seabed
imagining butterflies shattered by silence   their silkiness shredded
magnificent moonset between a smoothing-out of pages
imagining   the rustle of a pen-nib dipped deep in ash as it writes
a storm forced to become a one-beat pause in history
cello bows have been drawn over strings   light splattered out

a non-existent now increasingly a now with no beginning or end
silent after shattering

童年地理学

录进雪白墙壁的笑声　播放给谁听
高大明净的玻璃窗　留给哪阵风
别处的夏季远至另一种鸟鸣
阳台的站台　擦拭得海拔亮晶晶
回头　才看见喷水池和小沙坑
都上紧发条　秋千荡向出生的梦
梦见他盛在手提篮子里启程
像丢了　彩色的皮球拍进云层

落下时　绿荫的耳膜上粘满了蝉
吓人的爆发把更吓人的茫然
堆到他脸上　照片攥紧这瞬间
一种空空的凝视像突然瞥见
土地的敌意也已半岁　抓住这双眼
他不懂的血缘拉开铁路的拉链
把隧道那头的房子推得更远
他不懂的距离　刚刚起源

唉　换韵把镜片后结冰的德语
变成京剧中烫人的大红大绿
换了　胶纸背后渗出棕黄的影子
他发愣　犹豫　而母亲的剪辑
演奏大半生才微微显出深意
还在继续安顿他　还用手遮着隐没的
门牌　唉　母亲　他终于被允许
因为爱你　使用祖国这个错字

Childhood geography

recorded in the laughter of a snow-white wall   to whom broadcast?
high windows of bright glass   left for what breeze or gust?
elsewhere's summers arrive from afar at another kind of birdsong
the balcony's station platform   scrubbing sea level till it gleams
turn around   to see the fountain and the little sandpit
speeded-up clockwork   swings rocking to a dream of being incarnate
dreaming he set out on his way carried in a hand basket
as if lost   a coloured ball slapped into the cloud's jacket

when it falls   the green shade's eardrum is sticky with crickets
that terrifying eruption piles on his face a more terrifying vacancy
more terrifying   the photo seizes this moment
a blank stare as if suddenly glimpsing how
the earth's hostility is six months old now   capturing those eyes
blood ties he doesn't understand unzip the railway line
push the house at the end of the tunnel far far away
a distance he doesn't understand   has only just begun

oh   a change of rhyme freezes the German tongue in the camera
into the scaldingly bright reds and greens of Peking Opera
exchanging   russet shadows that ooze from the back of gummed paper
he dozes   hesitates   and mother's editing
only shows its delicate depth once half his life is acted
still settling him down   her hand obscures the disappearing
door number   oh   mother   at last he is permitted
because he loves you   to use the misprint 'motherland'

王府井——颐和园

一阵风就吹裂春水　　哪怕它绿遍千载
投井妃子的一颗颗珠宝嵌着媚态
漂流的湖面上　　毒酒又斟满了玉杯
皇帝被一扇比丝还软的虚词屏风隔开
囚死之美太优雅　　太贵　　太颓废
公子哥儿用一个手势输给奴才
泥地上跪出的小坑渗漏嫩嫩的膝盖
风声依次把一盏盏宫灯掐灭

从东华门出去　　梅兰芳窈窕的尾音
甩着他　　前朝的海棠花和柏树林
沿着红砖墙的平行线为倾圮押韵
按下快门就是世纪　　照片上的鬼魂
眨眼　　吸走浸湿每个光圈的阴
历史的导游图错开一步　　淫艳如内心
倒扣一只乌鸦抵消的不真实的人群
从神武门出去　　小贩叫卖着黄昏

一只金丝雀藏在体内的音叉　　惊动
湖岸的曲线　　荷花的睡意　　知春亭
换一艘炮舰（谁写的？）　　该庆幸风铃
航程更远　　垂柳的弦乐拂去海浪的冷
太后　　办了敢阻挡玉如意的　　倘若可能
也在子宫里办了他　　罚那假象牙的天空
隐身的鸟爪在灰蒙蒙水面上邀请
他的柳絮迎向另一个时间　　疾掠匆匆

Wangfujing – Summer Palace

a breeze splits the spring spate   though it's the millennium's greenest
coquetry set with every jewel of a concubine who threw herself in the fountain
on the lake's drifting face   poisoned wine has filled a jade bumper
the emperor cut off behind a screen of empty words softer than satin
the beauty of dying in jail too elegant   too noble   too decadent
with a gesture the princeling loses to the bondservant
kneecaps in the rutted knee-worn mud oozing-tender
palace wicks snuffed out in sequence by the noise of the wind

exit the Gate of Eastern Glory   the final syllables of Mei Lanfang's sweet singing
swing him into   the last dynasty's crab-apple blossom and cypress groves
follow parallel lines of red-tiled walls that rhyme with toppling
it's the century releasing the shutter   the soul in the photo
blinks   sucks up the dark soaking into every f-stop
history's tourist map misses its step   seductive as the innermost soul
inverts the untrue crowd that is controverted by a single crow
exit the Gate of Divine Might   pedlars hawk the gloaming

a tuning fork hidden in the canary's body   startles
the lake shore's curve   the dozy lotus blossoms   Realising Spring Pavilion
exchanged for a gunboat   (who wrote that?)   chimes that ought to be cheerful
a farther voyage   weeping willow strings strum away the waves' chill
the Empress Dowager   did for those who resisted her sceptre   if she could
and did for him in the womb too   punishing the mock-ivory firmament
concealed bird claws on dark dusky water call on
his catkins to welcome another time   too quickly gone

二姨的肖像

西北风拧紧窗户上一千朵冰花
窗帘还黑着　雪的黑沙子响在她脚下
四合院的五点钟　黎明是一幅石板画
细部一　一侧发亮的手指得得叩打
男孩子粘着梦的玻璃映出一头白发
细部二　烤得热乎乎的馒头包进手帕
热热的目光送他上学　咳嗽声篦着朝霞
细部三　遗容似的天空靛青如一块蜡

记忆　再多笔触也画不出一幅肖像
只记得她骨灰盒移走的那天　房间多空旷
真走了　一个咽下矮矮身影的远方
哭喊不能　而一卷手抄的诗能追上
拽着那衣襟像拽着一锅荷叶粥的清香
墓穴下　字的调皮鬼紧挤在她身旁
还要跟她睡　当他又故意把儿子笑嚷
成"蛾子"　一滴泪烫着黑暗　嗤嗤响

伟人们相信青铜像　她的伟绩却是一条线
划定在他眼里　小胡同追着时代更换
坡度　而拆开的旧毛裤在她织针间
加热　善良竟如此简单如此难
像个重负得忍着　一件老羊皮袄的蓝布面
忍住更多早晨　他醒来仍捧着那张脸
从自己海底捞起　被洗净的贝壳缀满
一只古朴的石锚稳稳系着他的船

Portrait of Auntie

north-west winds screw thousands of frost-flowers on the windowpane
the curtain still blackening   her feet crunch black grains of snow
five o'clock in the four-square courtyard   daybreak a litho print
detail #1   a slant and shining finger raps tock-tock
a boy's dream-sticky glass reflects a head of hoary locks
detail #2   steamed rolls piping hot and wrapped in a handkerchief
a warm gaze sends him off to school   coughs comb the rosy dawn
detail #3   the death-mask sky a candle-like indigo

memory   more and more brush strokes can't paint a portrait
all I remember is the day her urn was taken away   the room so bare
really away now   a distance that swallowed that low silhouette
weeping and wailing can't   if a hand-copied book of poems can chase her
tugging at a lapel like tugging at lotus-leaf gruel's faint aroma
beneath the open grave   naughty ghosts of words squeeze in beside her
still needing to sleep next to her   as again he makes his son howl with laughter
turning into a 'moth'   one teardrop scalding the darkness   the sound of rupture

great men put trust in brazen images   her great feat was a thread
delineating inside his eyes   the little lane that changed shape as it chased
times   between her needles the old long underwear unravelled
and got warmer   kindness really is that simple and that hard
like a burden that must be borne   the blue cotton of the old leather coat
bears even more mornings   he wakes still cradling that face in his hands
dredged up more of his own sea bed   decked with new-washed shells
his boat is steady and safe chained to a simple anchor stone

不一样的土地

一个人必须习惯死亡的念头
五十岁　厌倦从一群绿头鸭的颤抖
传染到水珠里　滴滴亮晶晶的油
涂抹母亲枯木色的掰不开的手
他被铆住　按向黄白多皱的井口
看　童年的狗尾草狂奔着渐渐生锈
尖声唱的河面被月光的倒钩
提着　一串青蛙腿剥皮后的肉

鲜活如菜谱中炖了千年的美味
磨秃一把把勺子　火炉旁躬下的背
保姆们的慈祥在树梢血脉里轮回
围裙飘飘围护一簇桃花安睡
而坟头压着的纸片和一块小石碑
被一场雨漂白　洁净的子宫没有字
却和地平线教给他一样多　蓄着水
二胡声高涨成孩子漆黑的水位

周年　注射进一只苹果
考古学的黄色掌心板结在此刻
他回顾中总有西山淡紫色的轮廓
膝盖上一只小黑狗信赖的眼珠盯着
自己被吃掉　馋人的肉香像在说
没有过去　才更新每一岁的化学
跟上雾中土粒中越搂越紧的死者
习惯　直到迷上　一种最耐咀嚼的苦涩

A different land

a person must get used to the idea of dying
at fifty   wearied by the mallards' trembling
infecting a drop of water   oil gleaming drip by drip
smearing on mother's hands the colour of dry unbreakable twigs
he is riveted   pressed into a wrinkled yellow-white well-head
sees   youth's foxtail grass bolting as it rusts away bit by bit
the squealing of the lake's song picked up on a moonlight
barb   skinned frog legs on a spit

delicacies fresh from a cookbook and stewed a millennium
grind every spoon smooth   backs bowed over the oven
the kindliness of nannies circulates though every branch and vein
aprons flapping in defence of peach blossom's sweet slumber
while the grave is weighted with paper and the little headstone
bleached by a shower of rain   no words in the spotless womb
but as much as the horizon taught him   storing water
the fiddle's swell a child's jet-black plimsoll line

anniversary   injected into an apple
archaeology's yellow palms instantly hardening
forever in his backward glance the mauve contour of the Western Hills
on his kneecaps eyes trusted by a little black dog are opening
he's being eaten away   the scent of glutton flesh like saying
there is no past   only then will chemistry remake each year of life
caught up with the dead squeezed tighter into mist and loam
used to   even fascinated by   the most cud-chewed suffering

姐姐

你后院里盛开的牡丹也系在一只蜘蛛
闪闪的丝线上　花瓣年年的尸骨
一次次粉碎于一个鲜艳的刻度
他的花棉袄是你穿旧的　紫竹院的小湖
停进春雨　你春水似的胳膊搂住
弟弟　莲叶间孤零零的亭子在驶出
他偷听到候鸟的小心房里血流多急速
紧贴身边　世界一如轻信的少女

你脸颊上粉红的蝴蝶也会唱
一首黑歌曲　被撕碎也有初恋的疯狂
一辆自行车飞驰进十六岁　你翱翔
历史骑着青春期的风力伸张翅膀
鼻息一层层磨损天空时那么烫
历史　叹息得像排黑土地上蹒跚的白杨
被死者肥沃　告诉你　哪片绿叫远方
哪儿是天边　被暴风雪锁在你脚上

躲着的回忆录干呕一口口墨汁
蜘蛛毛茸茸的指爪钩在胃里
一盆水仙花旁弟弟傻笑像个聋子
妈妈却听懂了　电报断断续续的口吃
血缘般刺耳　颤颤的网上残骸多精致
你为那些你发育成不哭叫的故事
鬼魂的盲文缀满牡丹重叠的肉色
当所有噩梦　连这几行　不小心都是史诗

Big sister

the peonies in your backyard are tied to a twinkling
spider's web   the petals' annual skeletons
shatter one by one in colour-blazing calibrations
it's his hand-me-down padded jacket you wear   Purple Bamboo Park's pond
anchored in the spring rains   your arms like spring tides enfolding
a little brother   the lonely pavilion among the lotus leaves is leaving
how quick flows the blood he hears in the chambers of the migrant bird's heart
pressed against her   the real world like a young girl who's too trusting

the pink butterflies on her cheeks can also sing
a black song   ripped to shreds along with first love's folly
a bicycle speeding into sixteen   you circle and soar
history stretches its wings riding youth's wind-power
breath so hot it wears the sky away layer by layer
history   sighs like the limping poplars lining the black loam
fertilised by the dead   telling you   what stretch of green is called far
where the horizon is   snow locked onto your feet by the howling gale

the recumbent memoir retches up ink by the mouthful
spider's shaggy paws hooked into the belly
by a bowl of narcissus a little brother giggles like a boy hard of hearing
but our mother understands   the telegram's intermittent stuttering
ear-piercing as consanguinity   how delicate the wreckage in the web trembling
for those stories that you grow into the story of not weeping and wailing
ghostly braille petal by petal embellishes the flesh tints of the peony
like every nightmare   even these lines   will become an epic if you're not careful

"一九五七年初春"

谁猜到　这一年已包括了许多年
水声响在皮肤下　水做的牌坊那边
冬天跺着脚　而一辆儿童车推进春天
一只温度计向下拉枝杈枯黄的花园
空气中拧紧的咸味儿　渗漏成照片
的灰　一簇等在南方的花蕾远隔时间
母亲亲手布置好一个吻聚焦的严寒
他被放在这里　眼神蛰疼地平线

水写的一行小字　被擦掉才完成那宿命
水看不见地继续剪辑冻红的鼻孔
风搜索某女孩正被分娩的血腥
一块绿琥珀挂在一丝飘来的啼哭中
两个零下两次嵌进西山的锯齿形
将锯疼同一片紫色　用回头看的眼睛
母亲亲手布置好花园里悬挂的一秒钟
还没到来就过了　这约会的空

自始就在玩小小乳名里的不完美
这一年植入许多年　这干透的水池
被一个对水声的想象慢慢搓碎
他坐着的岸延长　他奔跑的小腿
奔入木本的处境　钉死在抽芽的刺痛内
肉的粉红色运载一枚石质的蕊
母亲亲手布置好鸟儿笔直掷来的手雷
眼睛里的融雪　突然原谅了无知

'Early Spring 1957'

who'd have guessed   how many more years this one year would hold?
sound of water beneath skin   those water-built memorial arches
winter stamps its feet   and into spring a pedal car pushes
thermometers pull down a garden of withered yellow branches
salty tastes wrung from the air   leak on to the grey tones
of the photo   clusters of southern buds remote from time
mother's own hand sets up a bleak kiss-focused cold
he was put here   his expression a bee-stung skyline

line of little words written on water   that destiny fulfilled when it's wiped away
water goes on unseen cutting and compiling cold-reddened noses
wind searches out some girl with the bloody reek of parturition
a lump of green amber hangs in a wail on the wind
two below zeros twice set in the sawtooth of the Western Hills
a saw to spoil the same purple patch   eyes look around
mother's own hand sets up one garden-hanging second
still not here, yet gone   the emptiness of this assignation

playing imperfection in a tiny baby-name from the beginning
this year planted in many others   a dried-up pond
slowly crumbled by imagining the water's sound
his little running legs   stretched by the bank he sits on
rush into the tree roots' quandary   crucified in a budding stab-wound
pink of flesh delivering a small stone-built stamen
mother's own hand sets up a grenade the birds flung round
melting snow in the eyes   ignorance instantly forgiven

"虎子"

你缩进角落一声声呕着叫
呕　血味儿的委屈　血淋淋撒娇
像个语言循着太空中幽暗的轨道
固定孩子眼里夺命的最后一跳
一堵破砖墙上食肉的刃立着切削
受宠的一生　乱石的流星雨乱扔下问号
两束鳄鱼绿的目光加九条命　你能逃
到哪儿　一件鼠类的血衣已织好

今夜　张挂到你猩红的身体里
一张猩红的小嘴翻开一部传记
让一团小肉舔着奶　一根舌头满是刺
每天早晨蹲上枕头痒痒舔醒孩子
一只虎酷爱虐待自己的龙凤尾
你的野　无愧春夜的朕　呼喝成群妻妾
你的愚蠢是非把一个热被窝钻到底
信任的鼻尖沁凉像个生僻的词

蒸发到国家里　焚烧押着韵
猫的阶级遭遇猫的斗争　通缉逼近
他的手也背叛了　你被抱出门的一瞬
眼神是人的　眼底有个模糊的母亲
早早咬断脐带　丢下一小撮灰烬
一次捣毁终于抵达驯练成熟的残忍
骸骨上　风拨动枯干的毛　阴魂
保持报复性的弱　针尖一样细细呻吟

64

'Little Tiger'

you shrink into a corner bawling and bawling
vomit   the nuisance of blood's stink   a blood-soaked tantrum
like a language following its dark orbit through the vacuum
deciding the last fatal leap in the child's eye
on the rubble wall the carnivorous blade is cutting
a pampered life   a stone meteor shower throws question marks at random
two crocodile-green gazes plus nine lives   you can run away
to where   your bloody rodent coat has been knitting

tonight   hung inside your scarlet body
a tiny scarlet mouth flips through a biography
lets a little ball of flesh lap milk   tongue all spiky
kneels each morning on the pillow to tickle and lick the scarlet child awake
tiger passionately in love with the illustrious tail that abuses it
your wilderness   worthy of this spring night's Royal We   shouts crowd the seraglio
deep into the warm duvet your stupid quarrels burrow
nose-tip wet and cold as an uncommon word yet trusty

evaporated into the state   rhyming with incineration
the cat class met the cat struggle   the arrest warrants drew close
his hands betrayed too   the instant you were carried through the door
the cat's look is human   deep in his eyes mother is a misty blur
she long ago bit off the umbilical cord   only a pinch of ashes left
cruelty shattered once reaches a trained maturity at last
on a skeleton   the wind ruffles dry hair   the departed soul
keeps an avenging weakness   a pinpoint-fine moan

水中天

水是假的　　天空也是　　这彩绘
比皮肤还薄　　画上就等着被撕毁
搬空的房间里有他回声似的十五岁
一捆书　　死死包扎一场假寐
一张拆掉的床像不知道归期的杜子美
再不猜测归期　　倒映的云暗黄浅黑
拧出淋漓的历史　　他听见池塘的嘴
说　　家是假的　　一根手指就搅碎

爸爸的颜色　　呛死窗户的革命
把一只铜制的高音松鼠拴在五点钟
歌唱　　姑妈上吊的脸俯向他晃动
像砍倒的西府海棠　　只许水下的风
嗅她枝头的幽香　　深深藏进距离中
姐姐是一只雁　　返回的羽翎
触着水面被取消的方向　　梦
见　　二姨悄悄抽泣　　弟弟傻呆呆发愣

十五岁　　水中的家用尽了时间
他的天空什么是谎言　　什么不是谎言
学会潜泳的呼吸本身已是条弃船
用哐啷摔死的门　　锁住留下来的黑暗
所有日子的假留在他回不去的那天
不可能更真了　　黄昏被水底俯瞰
不可能没有海风的内心　　冷而艳
海鸥叫着　　他的残余抵押给了盐

66

Sky in water

water is untrue   so is sky   these coloured patterns
thinner than skin   once painted wait to be dismembered
his fifteen years like an echo in an empty chamber
a book bundle   a tightly-wrapped catnap
a broken bed like Du Fu not knowing the day of return
won't guess when again   inverted clouds grey and umber
wring out a soaking history   he hears the pond's mouth
say   home is untrue   it's pulverised and disposed of at a touch

Father's colour   revolution that choked the window
at five o'clock hangs a bronze squirrel soprano
singing   Auntie's hanged face swinging as she bent over him
like crabapples cut down in the Western Palace   letting only the submerged wind
smell her faint perfume on the branches   deep hidden in distance
Big Sister is a wild goose   feathers of homecoming
beating in the direction water cancelled   dreaming
seeing   Second Aunt silently sob   Little Brother blankly dozing

fifteen years old   the family in the water   all their time spent
in his sky what is falsehood   what is not falsehood
to have learned underwater breathing is to be a ship abandoned
with the door banging like a fatal fall   locking up the leftover dark
the untruth of all the days left in that day he can never revisit
can't be truer   twilight is overlooked by the riverbed
cold and lovely   it can't not have the sea breeze's heart
seagulls cry   what's left of him has been mortgaged for salt

照相册之三：

1974. 5. 4——1976. 1. 7.

中国，北京。

PHOTOGRAPH ALBUM 3

4th May 1974 – 7th January 1976

Beijing, China

诗章之三：鬼魂作曲家

这一次性归纳烫伤的结构
不像空间　　而像空聚精会神
手指揉弄　　大海的磷光刮疼脸颊
一场奔流奔赴乌有的流向

这鬼魂摸黑编织的结构
停在它自己的无限里
音符高擎一朵朵荷花

在他体内看不见的太空中爆开焰火
在五月娇艳的石拱顶下
一个老人的骨骼是一把木椅子
吱嘎作响　　靠着墙
抱紧孩子们稚嫩的一刹那

五月　　胎盘里遍布雨声
为每只耳朵把孤独再发明一次

把一朵郁金香鼓胀的乳头再吮一下
他见惯的垂死　　让眼眶更娇嫩
他被过滤的血肉淹没了春色
斟入大提琴婉转的腰身
吱嘎作响

空　　拨动
房间里一只阳光的节拍器
哼声总是最后一次　　遗言摩擦
历史呛进一具躯体总在自己那次
鬼魂的指尖熔化滴落
一小节一小节山河搁在聋哑的位置上
归纳精美的　　非人的仪式
一枝羽毛笔永不谢幕
写下无处去进一步流失
唱啊　　世界就学会这样存在

Canto 3: Ghost Composer

                    this structure sums up scalding in one
                    unlike space   but like emptiness listening rapt
fingers kneading   ocean phosphorescence painfully scrapes face and jaw
the current races towards nothing

                    this ghost structure woven of blackness
stops at its own limitlessness
musical notation lifts each lotus blossom

fireworks explode in an unseen interplanetary space inside him
under the ravishingly lovely stone arches of May
an old man's skeleton is a wooden chair
creaking   leaning against the wall
tightly hugging that instant when children are young and tender

May   sound of rain all through the placenta
rediscovering loneliness for every ear

so take another suck at the tulip's swollen nipple
his familiar dying   makes the eye sockets more fragile
his filtered flesh and blood drowns spring's colours
pouring into the cello's melodious waist
creaking

                    emptiness   in the room
strums the sun's metronome
moaning is always the final time   last words rubbing
history chokes on a body always at that time of its own
ghost fingertips melt and drip
bar by bar the land is left on the deaf-mute's seat
                    to summarise the exquisite   inhuman ritual
a quill pen never takes a curtain call
write no place to run further away
oh sing   like this the world will learn to be

黄土南店，一九七四年五月四日

老白马的腰扭得好看　　每一颠
扑鼻一股膻味儿　　马车擦过麦田
甚至没惊动刚没膝的绿色
五月　　阳光和土都很慢

慢慢拆散一条路泛白的语法
记忆一碰就变大　　布谷鸟点播着片断
老白马知道那村子也是倒退的影子
隔着一道道吃力碾磨的坎

路边的白杨树也在慢吞吞倒叙
水沟　　坟头　　土坯墙像卷旧影片
放映在眼神里　　眼皮渗出日子的黄
西山昏睡成一列嵌着锦葵的宅院

那儿有扇木门　　像棵活的栗子树
攥紧小青果似的手　　受惊的嫩和软
那儿时间在叶子们的鱼群里垂钓
血咬了钩　　最古老的哲学仍是一声长叹

母亲送别时转身擦掉的泪
也是影子　　从记忆再错位一点
一头瞎了的老牲口就踅入春天的缝隙
他到了　　村名的绿锈爬满一张脸

Huangtu Nandian, 4th May 1974

the old white horse's back sways prettily   with every jolt
a rank stench fills the nose   the cart scrapes over cornfields
not even startling a just knee-high green
May   sunshine and soil both slow

slowly beheading the road's bleached grammar
memory enlarges with the collisions   cuckoo requesting morsels
the old white horse knows this hamlet is also a backward shadow
cut off from each and every laboriously milled hollow

roadside poplars in flashbacks excruciatingly slow
gutters   graves   mud walls like a rolled-up old movie-show
reflected in his eyes   eyelids leak the day's browns
the Western Hills doze into a courtyard inset with mallow

there's a wooden gate there   like a living chestnut tree
gripping little hands like olives   startled soft and tender
there time casts its hook into the shoal of verdure
blood takes the bait   the oldest philosophy still a deep sigh of grief

as Mother says goodbye she turns to wipe the tears away
and is a shadow   misplaced a little in recall once again
the old blind beast of burden pads into a crack in spring
he has arrived   over his face creeps the patina of the hamlet's name

一间喃喃毁灭箴言的小屋

柳树歪着脖子沉思一座池塘
泡着的死猫也像植物　　种下就膨胀
四季咸腥的丰收　　嗅着一间小屋
灌满水　　缩得更小　　在倒映出的方向

摸到一些嘴唇　　潜伏在油漆里
淤血的蓝色吻着就像锁着那门窗
三年了　　他听着咽喉下刹住的呼救
托起地面　　砖头渗出尸骨的阴凉

摸到一个集体的　　暴死的时间
不会结束的时间　　那雨声踩在瓦上
雨滴的银指头整夜测试一把镰刀的刃
再割下早晨时　　青草放肆的香

领着他　　跟踪鬼魂也有过的初恋
总在喃喃自语　　要坐进被掐灭的烛光
总能漏下更深　　一声西北风的口哨
吹着完成不了的迁入　　去想象

距离是用田野编织的　　人形的
目光从回顾叠压进回顾　　没有墙
没有间隔　　薄冰咔咔碎　　泥泞的燕子
被拴在地下几米　　他死死攥着重量

Room where mottoes of destruction are mumbled

willows tilt their heads to contemplate the pool
bloated dead cat like a vegetable   then puffed up after planting
a stinking harvest of four seasons   sniffing at a small room
poured full of water   shrunken smaller   along its reflection's bearing

touch the lips   in paint concealed
thrombosis-blue kissing like doors and windows sealed
three years now   he's heard in his throat a cry for help stuck
holding up the ground   the cool of dead bone seeping from brick

touch a time of collectivity   and of death without warning
time that will never end   the sound of rain on tiles treading
all night silvery raindrop fingers try the sickle's edge
the wanton smell of green grass   when morning is shorn again

leading him   in hot pursuit of the first love ghosts once had
always in mumbling   wanting to sit into the nipped-out candlelight
always able to leak more deeply   a whistle on the north-west wind
blows an endless immigration   into imagination

distance is woven out of fields   gazes in human likeness
folded in from looking back into looking back   there are no walls
no intervals   thin ice cracks and breaks   a muddy swallow
tethered many metres underground   he clings tight to heaviness

绿色和栅栏

田垄是金属的　　而他们佝偻的姿势
被铐着　　泥土的柔韧像一种鼓励
他们的裸背贴近玉米刀形的叶子
肋骨也每年一度油亮亮的绿

像一组埋进肉里的　　不会弄错的号码
一个酸涩的血型押送着麦粒
返回每年清明灌浆的　　被征集的颜色
遍地拔节的声音朗读着刑期

也有田园的风味　　渴的风味
命令井向一个零深处不停陷进去
他们蹲在井台上的茫然　　镶着田鼠
和鹌鹑　　一首地平线一样近乎色盲的诗

他们看不见子宫的咒语
仍在收缩　　一排绿色栅栏锁着呼吸
延伸到天边　　分蘖的晚霞仍黝黑
而无辞　活　监禁在一次静静的咀嚼里

端着的粗瓷碗　　平衡上了妆的岁月
什么也不意味　　连绿色的填空游戏
也不意味　揩着啐到脸上的一声喝斥
他们细细揩净一张犁

Green and fences

the field tracks were metallic   but these people's rickety deportment
is manacled   the mud's tough pliability like encouragement
their naked backs glued to the corn's knife-shaped tegument
and ribs each year a deeper shade of emerald sheen

like a set of numbers buried in flesh   that mustn't be miscalculated
a pungent blood group sending ears of grain under armed watch
returned to the called-up colours   the Days of the Dead in each year cemented
everywhere the sound of jointing crops reciting their jail stretch

with the taste of the fields and gardens   thirst's flavour
perpetually commands the well to fall to the depth of zero
these people squat by the vastness of a wellhead   implanting vole
and quail   a nearly colour-blind poem just like the skyline

they couldn't see the womb's malediction
still contracting   a line of green fences locking in breath
stretch to the horizon   sprouting sunsets still dark-skinned
and wordless   life   imprisoned in silent rumination

coarse china bowls held in both hands   balance the rouged and painted years
meaning not a thing   not even the game of filling in green blanks
has any significance   wiping the spittle of denunciation from their cheeks
how thoroughly and carefully they wipe clean their ploughshares

饥饿再教育

风只朝一个方向吹　　把他吹弯了
风声加剧那种空　　锤子凿刻
到胃里的空　　夜的流体
物质肆虐的水银色

观音土和榆树皮的传统在上课
他的教科书　　舔着被钩住的上颚
学习对一只麻雀无限的色情
喉头抽搐　　羽毛包裹的一股肉味混合

妄想的味儿　　天敌醒在他内部
秒针挑着暴风雨　　器官们的自我
否认他的自我　　马须草　　槐花　　水葫芦
两把野菜间碧绿的比较消化学

呕出一场说谎的酸液的洪水
擦得雪亮的灶台令孩子眼巴巴望着
刨不出月色的土地像笔糊涂债被欠着
一只回声叮当的铝饭盒

像位失去祭祀的神　　罚他专注
这事实　　这一阵肠子空转的折磨
他沿着累坏了的白薯藤追上
被开除的　　啃食着冷冷曙光的生活

Hunger re-education

the wind only blows in one direction   blows him crookback
the wind's howl intensifies the emptiness   a hammer hewing
at the emptiness in his stomach   night's juices flowing
matter's quicksilver raging and wanton

elm bark and Our Lady's Earth are still on the syllabus of famine
his textbook   licking the hook-caught jawbone
learning limitless lust for a sparrow
twitching in the throat   whiffs of feather-wrapped meat combine

the tastes of wishful thinking   inside him a predator stirs
the second hand choosing the storm   the ego of his innards
denies his own ego   horsebeard grass   water hyacinth   scholar tree
between two handfuls of wild herbs the green of comparative digestology

vomiting out an acid flood of deceit
the brightly-polished hob makes children helplessly stare
soil where moonlight can't be dug is owed like a senseless debt
the ding-dong echo of the aluminium lunch-box there

as if a god who'd lost his sacrifices   fined him for boiling down
this reality   this torment of empty guts grinding
he chases along the exhausted sweet potato vines
a life cashiered   spent chewing on a cold cold dawn

遗失的笔记本

那些纸是漆黑海水中不反光的鳞
粘在不反光的鱼脊上慢悠悠下沉
那张塑料脸颊溢出一首诗幼稚的香
越不会写的手越摸到一种深

还拉着一盏小灯　穿过满村狗吠
还守着田野的绿意　押错午夜的韵
一粒琥珀小小的恋情还向一次遗失
成熟　辞句的听觉热热封存

隔壁那声轻轻的带鼻音的咳嗽
指尖敲叩密码　窗棂间月色被刷新
等在一行白杨喧哗的针脚中　缝死了
回家梦　一朵肯定距离的云

在张贴他自己的　生疏的笔迹
那篇慢悠悠斜插入命运的盲文
让女孩毕生折射成水波　一页页颤抖
翻阅到底才剥出女人

有种和他同样的　不在的风度
有次未竟的沉没　母亲擒获的
敲门声也丢了　凭惊人递增的无色
遗失到血里的字终于可信

Lost notebook

these pages are non-reflecting fish scales in pitch-black brine
leisurely sinking while stuck to non-reflecting fish spine
from the plastic jaw leaks the naïve perfume of a poem
the less the hand can write the more it touches depths of some kind

still dragging a little lamp   through the village dogs' barking
still keeping to the fields' greenness   wrongfully arrested rhymes at midnight
love as tiny as a grain of amber still facing a one-off deprivation
to come to maturity   heat-seal the words and phrases' hearing

next door the quiet sound of nasal coughing
fingertips tap a code   between the astragals moonlight is redrawn
waits in the stitches of a roaring line of poplars   tightly sewn
a cloud a definite distance away   a dream of home-going

posting up his own   unpractised handwriting
that Braille slowly and crookedly inserted into his fortune
making a girl's whole life reflect as waves   page by page trembling
to read to the end will flay a woman

there is the same as his   a kind of non-existent ease
there is one incomplete sinking   the knock on the door Mother held
is also lost   thanks to greyness's amazing increase
words mislaid in the blood can be trusted in the end

水渠

村子也漂走了　薄如水彩的倒影
游过　黄昏的丝光憋死一种空
只有他能看见　用三十年后
一双潜回水底的眼睛

看着对土地的爱找到一个人形
看着那人远远走过　镜头里汩汩水声
拍摄十九岁清澈流淌的主题
赤脚上芬芳隐喻似的泥泞

记住一抹精雕细刻的湿
村子让穿着绿色水草的力挥动
他慢慢懂　七幅地　九江口　场院南
那人的绚丽分给珠串般的地名

一粒粒消失　乳头被吮过的娇艳
在水面折断　只有他看见河水多透明
一座十九岁架起的绞盘　绞至
旧照片怀抱的双重不在的冷

鸟儿探监似地盘旋在头上
心里流走越多世界　水渠的色情
越宁静　延伸一个梦的简单形象
三十年后缺口溃决　一声鸟鸣

Sewers

the village has drifted away too   thin as a watercolour reflection
swum past   twilight's sheen stuffs emptiness to bursting
only he can see   from thirty years after
with eyes that sneak back underwater

watching love of the land to find a human form
watching that person gone far away   in the lens water gurgling
photographing the nineteen-year-old motif of limpid flowing
fragrant mud on bare feet like metaphor

remember a smear of precision-made dankness
the village brandished by a power that wears green rushes
he slowly understood   Seven-Bolt Lands   Nine-Streams Mouth
                                        Threshing-Floor South
her beauty shared out to place-names like a pearl necklace

speck by speck lost   a sucked nipple's beauty so enchanting
snapped on the water   only he sees how transparent the rivulet
a nineteen-year-old capstan   winding
up to the doubly non-existent cold hugged by an old snapshot

like prison visitors above his head birds are circling
the more that worlds flow from his mind   the more sewer sex
calms down   extends the simple image of dreaming
thirty years on a bird's song   it bursts through the cracks

一张畏惧寒冷的狗皮

一张畏惧寒冷的狗皮　　久久
忍着钉子　墙在走　灰尘在走
你小心掩埋的死后也没有主人
雪在走　　雪上结了硬壳的月光在走

他穿过入夜的田野　　回来看
时间也不要的　　一只碎玻璃窗的漏斗
漏下不变的　　你的欢快发射到村边
又疯进屋里　　尾巴的旗语挥舞

受宠的音乐　　湿热的鼻孔喷着
搁上总有一本书摊开的膝头
母亲的信和一双盯紧他脸庞的眼睛
是仅有的烛火　　刻进劳累的梦呓的宇宙

但小小的恒温已经在说谎
你奔跑　叼着谋杀者垂涎的肉
四条黑丝绒的小腿苦苦等到了
一个剖开成平面的　　丢尽血味的深度

展览墙上一块灰尘勒边的白
畏惧了自己能被借用和剥下的天性
他听见那呼救　　渗出空房间的空
雪上满是牙印　　你不放弃的疼在复仇

A dogskin dreading the cold

a dogskin dreading the cold   long
long suffered nails   walls gone   dirt gone
your carefully-buried afterlife has no master
snow gone away   crusted moonlight on the snow gone

he passed through nightfall fields   came back to watch
what time didn't want either   funnel of windows breaking
leaking unchanged   your joy radiates to the village's end
running crazy through the rooms   tail's semaphore wagging

cherished music   humid nostrils spurting
put on knees where a book is always open
Mother's letters and eyes fixed on his face
the only candle flame   carved into a universe of dog-tired sleep-talking

it has been telling lies   the tiny thermostat
you run   in your mouth the meat killers covet
four little black velvet legs bitterly anticipate
a depth slashed open and flattened   depth of blood-stench lost

a white space exhibited on the wall by dusty reins
dread of your own self can be instinct borrowed and flayed
he hears the cries for help   oozing from the emptiness of the rooms
the snow is all tooth marks   the pain you didn't forsake takes its revenge

诗学

飘雪的日子最像一页诗稿
每个字是只小动物　玲珑的触角
没用过就钝了　一下午的心渐渐揉皱
渐渐濡湿成泥土　那所灰暗的学校

拉响蚯蚓们柔韧悠长的上课铃
青蛙勤奋掘进着冬眠的甬道
田鼠的眼珠　一对囤积星空知识的小贼
扮演老师监视麦粒中作弊的分秒

冒着严寒　尖尖的乳房也不忘灌浆
女孩如一朵等在羞涩里的棉桃
西北风记住所有约会　当冻红的手指
碰着手指　他那滴酒斟出一件古陶

他向大地学习细小的事情
细小的联系　心动一刹那唤回一只鸟
狗儿炖熟的泪水循环到他眼里
情人的身体香　像某种哭叫

心只动了一下　揪着卧在天边的山
暮色盛满寒冷的听力　寒冷的远眺
摆上小炕桌　他爱上不停开始的
第一场雪　飘落得如此姣好

Poetics

days of drifting snow most resemble a page of draft poetry
each letter a little beastie   nimble antennae
blunt if unused   the whole afternoon's heart slowly crumples
soaks steadily into the mud   that sombre academy

ring a drawn-out and pliable school bell for the worms
frogs struggle to dig hibernation's burial vault
the vole's pupils   little bandits hoarding knowledge of the stars
playing at teachers to oversee sham seconds and minutes in the corn

facing severe cold   pointed breasts don't forget mortar
a girl like a cotton boll waiting in modest reserve
north-west winds remember every tryst   as red frozen fingers
meet fingers   his wine drops pouring from an ancient jar

from the great earth he learns tiny delicate things
tiny delicate relationships   a bird calls back the instant of a heart leaping
a dog's long-stewed tears recycle back into his eyes
the aroma of a lover's body   like some kind of loud weeping

the heart leaps only once   grabs the mountains at the sky's end
twilight colours stuffed with a cold sense of hearing   cold far-off stares
at the little bed-table   he falls in love with the endlessly-beginning
first snowfall   so prettily falling and drifting

死·生：一九七六年

他一天天追赶母亲的死
追　一部早晨狂转的手摇电话机
自行车把顶着天空的噩耗后退
风砸在脸上　钢印砸进他的缺席

医院的味儿半握在蜡制的掌心里
母亲发脆的手　水泥地上摔断的树枝
带走了肩轴疼　磕坏的眼镜片
也在抱怨他来得太迟

或太早　一根蜡烛还得等三十年
完成那熄灭　那薄薄皮肤下黑暗的构思
逆着风佝偻蹬车　用字攻占一团果肉
三十年　缺席分娩他成一首诗

母亲一行也没读过的　一次次托梦
错过的　一种血脉滴洒墨汁
给一本蜡制的书无数早晨的篇幅
他星星点点洇开　像母亲隐秘发育的无知

用自己重写母亲诀别的年龄
自行车铃声似的死亡念头　太熟悉时
比事实还近　从碎了的骨灰瓮开始
他只剩双倍的生命和美丽

Life/Death: 1976

day after day he pursues Mother's death
chases   a hand-cranked phone that spins crazily in the morning
a bicycle forces the sky's worst-ever news into retreating
wind strikes his face   steel stamps strike home his absence

hospital smell half-held in a waxen palm
Mother's brittle hand   a broken branch fallen on concrete
took away her shoulder pain   smashed spectacle lenses
also complain he came back much too late

or too early   a candle must still wait thirty years
to be snuffed out   under that thin skin darkness's undertaking
pedals crookback against the wind   to attack fruit pulp with words
thirty years   absence gives birth to him as verse-making

Mother never read a single line   over and over in my dreams asking
and missing   black ink drips from artery and vein
extends a waxen book into endless morning
his scrappy blots   as Mother secretly grows her unknowing

with himself he rewrites Mother's age at the last farewell
the bicycle-bell-like thought of dying   when it's known too well
begins with a broken cremation urn   is nearer than reality
he is left with only double the life and double the beauty

照相册——有时间的梦

千分之一秒的现实都迎着赝品的未来
村子也夹进两页间　　小虫的残骸
多年前就碎了　　抱着他痛哭的光速
到封面为止　　母亲签署的水位

仅仅是这个名字　　玻璃幽闭的一夜
灯下米黄色拢住的日期被翻开
河水　　有个呛入鼻孔的硬度
他轮流被拧亮　　轮流墨绿地潜回

一帧深似一帧地制作一个梦
脸　　陷进粘合它们隔绝它们的空白
碾平的村子推着母亲碾平的阴户
抽啊　　时间的耳光一记记剪裁

每一帧溺死的经历　　每种赝品式的
青春　　雁声一夜夜呼啸着不在
鲜艳如一首序曲演绎的界限
仅仅需要界限　　一一检阅这溃败

都一样远　　母亲的断壁残垣
被他抱着　　还用一条发黄的路回家
这部把灰烬精美装订成册的家
千分之一秒后　　才懂得不醒来多么宝贵

Photo album – Dream in time

at a thousandth of a second all realities face a future of faking it
the village is squeezed between two pages   insect remains
broken long years ago   hug the light-speed he bitterly bemoans
until Mother signs the water level   on the book jacket

only this name   one night immured in crystal
beige-gathered calendars leafed through by lamplight
river water   solid enough to clog a nostril
he is switched on in turn   sneaks dark-greenly back in turn

a frame deep as any other frame manufactures a dream
face   falls into the blank that fused and severed them
the flattened village pushes at Mother's flattened pudenda
oh take it   again and again time's clout crops them

every drowned experience   every imitation
youth   night after night wild goose voices whistle non-being
colours bright as the edge of an overture's deduction
needing only an edge   to inspect these defeats one by one

all equally far away   Mother's ruined remains
embraced by him   still going home on a road that's yellowing
this home bound so exquisitely into an album
for a thousandth of a second only   he understands how precious is not waking

第二部

水薄荷哀歌：无时间的现实

（极慢的慢板）

PART 2

WATERMINT ELEGY: TIMELESS REALITY

(*Adagio pianissimo*)

水薄荷叙事诗（一）

——现实哀歌

WATERMINT NARRATIVE 1

Reality Elegy

履带下血红的泥泞
是
　　　一月的梅花还是六月的槐花？
钢铁缝隙间挤出一张脸的茫茫
　　　旋入石头的漩涡
当你走过不会绊住你的脚步
当你突然记起　甚至有一缕幽香
　　　甜甜绞着喉咙
当季节复印一片片碾平的花瓣
　　　　　　　　让你不知死在哪次
　　哪个清明雨声不在缝合丝绸的眉眼
　　你的惊愕　"卟"地溅出时
　　　　　　　复数的第一次在偷听唯一一次
眼泪炎热而空洞
我们走过不会绊住我们的脚步
　　　　　　　当　裤脚下轮轴辚辚滚动

　　国关筒子楼里幽暗的甬道
　　永远开着灯　炒锅的黄昏
　　紧倚着公共厕所冻硬的黄昏
　　一月的瀑布冲走他梦中喊出的名字

　　北风抱着照像册痛哭
　　分娩般急切的死　顾不上羞耻的死
　　他追赶的年龄迎着母亲瞳孔中
　　放大又放大的雪花

六棱形晶莹的冷
藏进刷新病房的梅花雨
　　　　　震落如弹片的槐花雨
　　　　　　　　你是否能认出？
被否认的白撑胀年年滋长的白
　　被否认的肉体
　　　　　　凝结下水道中的凝视
　　　　　　　　你是否能认出？

blood-red mire under tank tracks
is it
      blossoms of January's plum or June's scholar-tree?
a face's vast expanse squeezed out from gaps between iron and steel
      spun into a vortex of stone
as you have taken the steps that can't enmesh you
as you suddenly remember   there's even a faint whiff of perfume
      a sweet noose around your neck
as the seasons photocopy every flattened and crushed petal
                      so that you don't know what time you died
      the sound of which Day of the Dead rain isn't sewing your silken eyes
     when your astonishment   splatters out with a gunshot's crack
        plural first times eavesdrop on the one and only time
tears blisteringly hot but empty
we have taken the steps that can't enmesh us
         as   rumbling axles trundle beneath trouser turn-ups

     in the College of International Relations dorm's dark corridors
     lamps are always lit   the frying-pan twilight
     leaning close on the frozen twilight of the public toilet
     January's waterfall flushes away names he shouted in dreams

     the north wind hugs a photo album and wails
     death eager as childbirth   death that can't cope with shame
     the age he pursues to face the ever-larger and larger
     snowflakes in the pupils of mother's eyes

a hexagonal diamond cold
hides in the plum blossom rain of the renovated sickroom
        scholar-tree blossom rain thunders down like shrapnel
                      do you recognise it?
      denied white bloats the white that year by year went on growing
        denied flesh
           conceals the sewer's gaze
                      do you recognise it?

我们是否能认出
围观的星星间

    （女巫说）成群轮回的亲人？
    被毁灭不尽的历史缔结为亲人
       一块黑色大理石墓碑深处
     母亲掠过　今夕何夕
     掠过　家庭辗转　履带辗转

    夜砸开小屋的窗户　田野盯着他
    回来找　炕桌上亮着的鬼火
    一个卡在碎玻璃间的初恋
    给地砖漫上薄薄的雪花的沙子

    倒映墙上一块耀眼的白斑
    小黑狗剥皮时的惨叫　被钉着
    继续惨叫　断壁残垣一如对称
    别人越看不见的越令他如醉如痴

离开的日子都是清明
雨滴细数
         雨滴内微雕成颗粒状的宇宙
    淋湿的白布条上字迹依稀
    玉砌台阶下垃圾堆星闪着校徽
          自行车腥臭的骸骨
绊不住你因为你不知死在哪次
月光失踪式的存在多次
       忘　性感女儿似地长大
    只有一个故事的生命让我们晕
    我们太多的故事　每本书
        夹着一枝含铅的紫丁香
不变的体积
不停抽出一株植物里
        更空虚的美
     再来　房间才空了　情人真的走了

do we recognise
between the rubbernecking stars
      (the witch said) relatives reborn together?
   judged by endlessly-destroyed history to be relatives
      in the depth of a black marble headstone
      mother brushes by   *lo, what night be this?*
      brushing by   the families turn   the tank tracks turn

   night bangs the little room's window open   the field stares at him
   coming back to find   a will-o-the-wisp lighting up the bedside table
   first love throttled among broken glass
   covering the floor bricks with the fine sand of snowflakes

   reflecting a dazzling white stripe on the wall
   little black dog screaming in pain as it's flayed   nailed
   still screaming in pain   remnant ruins like symmetry
   the less others can see the more he's astonished

days of parting are always the Day of the Dead
raindrops count down
         a grainy cosmos carved in miniature in each raindrop
   handwriting faint on wet white bandages
   school badge twinkles in the midden under the jade stair
                       the rancid skeleton of a bike
it can't enmesh you because you don't know what time you died
moonlight's many existences seem to be missing
      forgetting   grows like a sexy daughter
   only having one story in our life makes us dizzy
   our too many stories   every book
      holds a branch of leaden lilac between the pages
a never-changing volume
from one plant endlessly tugging
      a still emptier beauty
   coming back   the room empty now   lovers truly gone

死亡的戏剧扭歪了五官
一只黄铜门把手　攥紧
拎起满满一桶鲜牡蛎的那只手
满满一桶目光在霉烂的地毯上摊开

他打开的信箱有个偷换的名字
他以为是自己的地址　读出
鬼魂就布满舞台　斧劈时脑浆迸涌
悬颈时随风飘飘　总不乏激情

引爆碧蓝海面上一团镁光
照耀那远眺　一架楼梯录制下
死者死去多年后才被还回的笑声
哀伤地埋入他异国的自我

花瓣的眼泪
该惊愕花瓣的虚无
　　渗出广场稿纸的眼泪
　　该惊愕　一行诗蜕变的虚无
世界不多不少是块封死的石板
　　　　　　你该哭你的忘　我们忘了又忘
　　　　　　才配上哭这不动的动词
　　用不停的哭演绎不哭
　　用人性本来的潮湿
　　　　　　　　拒绝添加更多潮湿
蓝天开足马力驰过
　　　　　　　履带重申
所有死亡说到底无非一个私人事件
跺响孩子们金属的舞步
　　线民　卧底者　处境厂商　交待材料的花匠　老大哥
　　艾滋村　黑煤窑奴工　塔利班　裸体飞翔的玛格丽特
　　革委会　超级粉丝　G20　Ground0　盗墓者　搜查者
　　柬埔寨骷髅　人间蒸发者　杜撰日历的人　造句的人
　　我　任何人

100

the drama of death has twisted their faces

the brass door handle   grips tight

the hand that carries a full tub of fresh oysters

a full tub of sight spilt on the mouldy carpet

the letterbox he opens bears a substitute name

he thought it was his address   read it out

souls fill the stage   brains spurt out as the axe falls

hung by the neck to swing in the wind   never lacking passion

detonate a flash of magnesium on the blue sea

to light up the distant gaze   under the stair's recording

the laugh of the long-dead who have only now been returned

pathetically buried in his foreign self

the tears of the petals

should stupefy the nothingness of petals

    tears leaking from writing paper of squares

    should stupefy   the transformed nothingness of a line of verse

the world is no more and no less than a flagstone that seals up dying

        you should weep for your forgetting   we have forgotten and still forget

        only then will we join in the weeping for this verbless verb

    infer unweeping from endless weeping

    with original human moistness

            refuse to add yet more moistness

the blue sky speeds past at full tilt

        tank tracks repeat

all death is simply a private matter in the end

stamping the metal taps of children dancing

   CID   undercover agents   trouble factories   grassing gardeners

   AIDS villages   charcoal-kiln slaves   Taliban   Marguerite soaring naked

   Revolutionary Committees super fanboys G20   Ground Zero   grave-robbers

                           vandals

   Cambodian skulls The Disappeared inventors of calendars makers of

                          sentences

  me   anyone

回到表面总不太晚
一场雨携来河谷的幽暗
朝南的窗户都湿了　清苦的肖像
似曾相识中一株水薄荷静静伫立

野鸭橘红的脚蹼　蹬开他
水声簸着水泡的空心珍珠
绿的舌尖倒唱一首黯淡下来的挽歌
尼禄媲美杨广

水之茫茫
他蘸啊吮啊她开花的粘液
漂的手指　浸进月色和这首诗两个表面
一滴水之内的茫茫

虚构的哀悼凿穿一月和六月
蕊　时而梅花时而槐花
　　　　　　在无数卧室的特洛伊
　　　　　　　　空出一件扮演女性的白袍子
　　死者的月亮傍着簇新的牌坊
　　　　　　夜把玩它的形式
一架摆进周年的照相机拍下
不在
　　　和母亲镜框前的烛光一起
　　　　　　和钉牢一座城市的灯火栅栏一起
高高的亭子中
暴露着性交
　　　　　　原地陷进黑暗

　　没有诀别的诀别
　　在一座书写的桥上　看一条河
　　用无数自沉慢慢释放出浑浊
　　躲着钓鱼的人正被钩住上颚

it's never too late to go back to the surface
a rain shower brings the valley gloom
south-facing windows soaked   portrait of bitter clarity
like long standing watermint in former familiarity

the orange web feet of wild ducks   tread on him
the sound of water winnowing the empty pearls of bubbles
green tongues sing a dimming dirge backwards
Nero a rival for the wicked emperor of Sui

vast expanse of water
how he dips how he sucks at the snot of blossoming
floating fingers   soak into the surfaces of moonlight and this poem
the vast expanse in one drop of water

fabricated grief chisels through January and June
stamens   sometimes plum sometimes scholar-tree
            the Troy in endless bedrooms
                empties a white tunic play-acting the woman
    the moon of the dead stands by a brand-new memorial gate
        night fiddles with the shape of it
a camera set to anniversaries shoots on
                            ABSENCE
        with a single candle before mother's picture-frame
                with the railings of light that nail down a city
in a tall pavilion
laying sex bare
                        site stuck in the darkness

no final farewell for final farewells
on a bridge of writing   looking at a river
turbid with numberless self-drownings in slow release
someone hiding at the fishing gets a hook in the jaw

没有现在的辞
摆进石珊瑚里的三亿年摆在
他桌上　腐烂的独一无二
对应蓝天上一场静静精巧的解散

没有什么不被倒叙
倒映一匹冷冽水面的丝绸
满坡芒草的羽毛笔银光闪闪
毕生签署一种最耐嚼的寒意

没有别的绝对　除了盲目
爱上一个为自己虚构的理由
因此再写一首只对自己值得一写的诗
并被怂恿成它的造物

现实不是一个主题　一张
　　　　钢铁词语间挤烂的脸
　不是任何人的
　　　旗子的啪啪掌声已褪色为风声
　　　　　　　一顶帐篷搭过的地方
　　　　急急传递一碗水的地方
是这里吗？
　　　你的脚步　我们的脚步
　　　　　在金属雨声中湿湿粘粘狂奔的地方
是这里吗？
　　　　　　　　　但这里是哪里？
　这无人是哪里？
　　　　绊不住花瓣的日日清明
　　　　驱逐不知疲倦的嫩嫩生命
　　轮回之绿从未轮回出一只眼眶
　茫茫　梗在咽喉下
　　　　　　　　淡淡的紫色
虚构一个摇曳的姿势
最擅长一种流淌的幻象
　　　流　成　血肉的难熬的奇迹
一株水薄荷用一只粉扑擎着灰烬

there are no words for this moment
set in three hundred million year-old coral set on
his desk   a rotting one of a kind
matching in silence the exquisite dismissal in the blue sky

nothing that isn't flashback
to reflect a bolt of silk on chilly water
the quill pens of all the banking's beard-grass shine silver
a lifetime signing the tastiest chill in the air

no other absolute   but the blind eye
in love with the reason that is made up for yourself
so write a poem only worth writing to yourself again
provoked to be its own creation

reality is not a subject   one face
                mashed between words of iron and steel
  is nobody's
            the flag's handclapping fades with the sound of the wind
                        the place where a tent was pitched
                straightaway sent to the place of a bowl of water
is it here?
      your steps   our steps
                in the sound of metallic rain a place of wet and sticky running away
is it here?
                        but where is here?
      where is this *ABSENCE OF SOMEONE*?
            the daily Day of the Dead that can't enmesh the petals
            banished a tender life that knew no exhaustion
      reincarnated green from the never-reincarnated brings out an eye
      vastness   stuck in the throat
                    pale pale purple
fabricates a swaying pose
most expert in the fantasies of flowing
      flowing   turned into   the unendurable miracle of flesh
watermint holds the ashes in a powder-puff

一天没呕出那条履带　　一天就在活祭
　　海水汹涌的裂缝灌满盲音

"今夜　　我为自己　　为你　　为离开一哭"

　　　到惊愕之外
　　　继续死去

a day of not vomiting tank tracks   a day of living sacrifice
    the crack seawater surges through pouring into blind sound

'tonight   for myself   for you   for leaving   I weep'

    arrive beyond astonishment
    go on dying

水薄荷叙事诗（二）

——爱情哀歌

赠友友

WATERMINT NARRATIVE 2

Love Elegy

FOR YO YO

1　一个街名使一场爱情温暖回顾

一个街名使一场爱情温暖回顾
我们水味儿弥漫的所有徘徊
李河谷银灰的波纹搁在窗台上
银灰的亮度　　总能容纳更多的雨
一只骨灰瓮柔和得像一只子宫
我们走　　而两个酷似你我的小家伙
不耐烦被领着　　纵身越过栏杆
甜点似的目光就叠入水的好奇
天鹅投掷林立的雪白脖子
码头绕过迟钝的锈
笑声中船名开成一长串荷花
阳光之日常　　一如妄想
滤除水中孩子们应有的年龄
之不可能

这些字写在
二零零六年十月二十五日
数字　　除了水深能说明什么
一个街口上两只交叉的桨
不停划动的石头刹那
你和我视线一碰
天上疾走的　　总在卷起帷幕的云
认出一件穿错的黄色灯芯绒衣服
故国用垂柳的老绿追踪而来
耳机里大提琴响应漆黑作曲的海水
一场录制　　持续二十三年
给河加上梦中也在流淌的耳语
给一闪一闪的爱减去一个世界
一道台阶竞争着空
倾斜到深处

1 A street name makes a love look fondly back

a street name makes a love look fondly back
all our wavering permeated with the taste of water
Lea River valley's silver-grey rippling is set on the windowsill
silver-grey brightness   can always take more rain
a cremation urn soft enough to seem like a womb
we walk   and two little figures so like you and I
are impatiently led   leap over the railings
candy-sweet gazes folded into the river's curiosity
swans throw snow-white necks as dense as thickets
the harbour curls around slow-witted rust
boats' names open a bunch of lotus blossom in laughter
sunshine's routines   just like delusions
filtering out the ages that children should have in water
is impossible

these words were written on
October 25th 2006
the numbers   explain nothing but the water's depth
two crossed oars at a street corner
endlessly rowing instants of stone
your gaze and mine meet
clouds scurry over the sky   always rolling up the stage curtain
recognise a coat of yellow lamp-wick down worn by mistake
our native land stalks us with the old green of weeping willows
cellos in the headphones answer a sea composed in jet-black
a recording   lasting twenty-three years
adds the murmur into the river that flows even in its dreams
subtracts a world from love's shimmer and shine
a staircase competing to be empty
slants into the depths

我　　并不比岸边锯倒的老树桩上
青苔累累的年轮更懒
事实上我像唱片一样勤快
整天从一个房间响到另一个房间
整天叫你　　你不在家也叫
两个重叠的字反刍美食的奇迹
满屋花草熟读你楼梯上的脚步声
渐渐慢了　　一丛油绿的虎皮兰
静默下来纺织纹身的金线
横贯我们银亮亮的水
不屑拒绝两个还没成形的小家伙
追着自己永远不会成形的噪音
沥青一路粉碎到孩子从未诞生的
尽头　　被刮掉的血肉
把每页诗复制成挽歌

I   am *not* lazier than moss-encrusted growth rings
on the old sawn-off tree stumps on the riverbank
in fact I am as hard-working as a gramophone record
blaring from room to room all day
calling to you all day   calling even when you're not there
two overlapping worlds ruminating on a gourmet miracle
flowers that fill the room read and re-read your step on the stair
gradually slowing   a grove of glossy green tiger-skin orchids
quiet down as they they spin a tattoo of golden thread
bright silvery waters cross us
obliviously refuse two little unformed figures
chase their own never to be formed voices
tar on the road fragments into the never to be born children's
final end   scraped-away flesh and blood
copies every page of verse as an elegy

2　水薄荷传

一片水平坦　明亮　静静推开两岸
像曼德尔施塔姆的黑土地

一片水擦拭他留给世界的武器
娜杰日达的心　删去雪不能记住的词

伦敦的雨也记不住　你和我的脸
湿淋淋编织的筛子间　多少人已漏掉了
鬼魂的盐分染白一辈子操劳的灌木丛
他看见那些脑袋　每颗镶着小绢花
吊在各自挑选的白昼的钩子上
切断甚至是甜蜜的　一只淡黄色灯罩下
他活着也得学我们窃听水位在升高
有多少黑夜就有多少一九三七年

沃罗涅什　读音是一只冻红的苹果
收尸的白雪一个字母一个字母背诵出
死者梗在咽喉里的那行诗

娜杰日达的心　在地平线上远远移动
她呕着　大海用终点的韵脚呕着
不是死　不是恨　只是爱
　　　爱上　一部蓝色鼻息呼喊的传记

　　　锁定　一条从眼睛到眼睛的连线
如果没有你　谁知道一页草稿的灰
怎样继续焚烧　一双用围裙擦干的手
怎样脱下海浪　渐渐被时间铸成了青铜
我们的厨房延伸他们的旷野　倚着
闲谈的火　甚至十一月的寒风也不是空的
两只茶杯间起伏的深海　只为你嘴边
滑出一枚鱼鳞白的名字而存在
斜斜飘落的雪带着诀别的一瞥

2 Watermint's tale

smooth water   bright   silently opened shores
like Mandelstam's black earth

water wiped clean the weapons he left to the world
Nadezhda's heart   excised the words that snow can't recall

neither can London rain recall   your face and mine
so many people have leaked away   between soaking plaited sieves
ghostly salinity bleaches a shrubbery that worked hard all its life
he sees these heads   each one inset with silk flowers
hang on the hooks of their chosen days
severed, even sweet   beneath a pale yellow lampshade
he's alive and must learn we eavesdrop on the water rising
as many black nights as nineteen thirty-sevens

Voronezh   the pronunciation is an apple frozen red
the white snow of the corpse-collectors recites it letter by letter
the dead straighten lines of verse in their throats

Nadezhda's heart   shifting far away on the horizon
she vomits   the ocean vomits the rhymes of destination
it's not death   it's not hate   it's only love
        in love with   a blue biography that breathes and roars

        locking   a line from eye to eye
if not for you   who could know the ashes of one first draft page?
how to keep on burning   hands wiped clean on an apron
how to strip away the ocean waves   slowly cast in bronze by time
our kitchen stretches out their wilderness   lolling
by a chatty fire   even chill November winds aren't empty
the swell of an ocean between two teacups   only exists for
the name white as a fish-scale that slides from your lips
snow drifts down aslant to bring a glimpse of final farewells

"冷酷的柔情"　他说
一个麻醉在人生里的重量
如果没有你细细的鼾声测定
窗外的星期三　我们漂出多远了
一抹秋色不会是这样

一片不停涌到胸前的水　　不停
重申一条落叶飞舞的无人区的路
死者的数目庞大得自动缝合
一株水薄荷的纤细　谁是娜杰日达呢
有多少黑夜就有多少门政治的外语
心颤抖着为一首诗探监　谁不是娜杰日达呢

如果没有一个甩着马尾巴长发的
少女姿影　不停横过
那条早被拆除的大街
一阵雨声就不会从梧桐叶上打进星空
给"只好活下去"加上着重点
如果没有衬着座死火山的铅色海水
像个背景或血统　把柠檬放进你掌心
谁会察觉"太阳"一词被渐渐停用了
一架"淡紫色雪橇"冲向大地的精疲力竭
如果爱是一块冰　失去的湿润给它硬度
没有一只精选的　娇美的耳朵
聆听噩耗　并排的枕头怎么疼如船舷
神话形成于这么近的地方

我们的分秒　增添一坛花雕酒的粘稠
恰似沃罗涅什一杯浇进冻土的伏特加
晚会开到墓地里　亡灵狂欢
　　曼德尔施塔姆　只有妻子
　　能迷上我们精致发作的癫痫

在被撕毁　焚烧　拷打　蒸煮之后
在值得或不值得的疑问之后
水的棺盖上　水薄荷砸着长长的钉子

a callous tenderness   he says
the weight has been anaesthetised in a life
if not for your delicate snore determining
Wednesday outside the window   we have drifted so far out
a smear of autumn colour can't be like this

water endlessly avalanches down our breasts   endless
restating of a street in no man's land where falling leaves flutter and dance
the number of dead so vast it's automatically sewn up
watermint's tenuosity   who is Nadezhda?
as many black nights as the foreign languages of politics
the heart trembles for a poem's prison visit   who isn't Nadezhda?

if not for one ponytail-swinging
girl's looks   endlessly crossing
that long-demolished avenue
the sound of rain on sycamore leaves couldn't have breached the starry sky
to *you have to go on living* it added marks of emphasis
if not for the lead ocean that lines the dead volcano
like lineage or background   putting a lemon in your hand
who could perceive the word *sun* slowly fall out of use?
a *lilac sledge*   charges toward the earth's weary exhaustion
if love is an ice cube   the lost moisture gives it hardness
there's no carefully-picked   ravishing ear
heeding the saddest of news   how can pillows abreast hurt like a ship's side?
a myth takes shape in places so close at hand

our minutes and seconds   thicken the jug of rice wine
like a glass of Voronezh vodka poured on frozen ground
the party drove to the graveyard   carnival of departed souls
        Mandelstam   only wives
        could be infatuated with our gently-breaking seizures

after being torn up   burned   tortured   digested
after deserved or undeserved suspicions
on the wooden coffin-lid   watermint collided with long iron nails

他和我混合的那撮灰亮晶晶递给你
才发现忍受一个诗人比忍受一首诗难多了

唯一的过去开始于伦敦一阵细碎的雹子
被人听见　因为河床疯子般失控
那深处北极光喃喃低语

the pinch of ash that mingled her and me is given glittering to you
only then to find that enduring a poet is much harder than enduring a poem

the only past begins in a London shower of hailstone fragments
heard   because the riverbed is as out of control as a lunatic
the murmur of an aurora borealis in the depths

3 一九八九年十月九日，纪念日

人生的决定　时而太难时而太容易
这租来的房间板墙幽暗
如一张冲洗过众多影像的负片
定影液浸泡着一场婚礼
我和你　衣衫洁净得像刚被你
浆洗过的旅馆床单
闵福德　邓肯　斯图尔特
三个朋友带来香槟与花
十月诡异的春色　点燃
街对面一棵蘑菇形的小树
这是奥克兰　草地上镶嵌着生命
证婚人的栏目里一笔一划写下
一片世界上最湛蓝的海

每个没参加婚礼的亲人的脸
都在那里　火山灰染黑的沙滩
张挂一排巨浪冷艳的虹膜
早等在这里　长长的下坡路像支历史的
针剂　给我们注射错乱的季节
让老房子油漆剥落的粉红色
追上风暴里一顶帐篷　锁住的白云
锁入窗框中天空的时速

我们的晕眩也发育成一个事件
恰如爱漫过每一夜的悬崖
一场回头张望　推我们没完没了
纵身一跳　这个日期里
鬼魂的羊齿草鲜嫩肥绿
非得借两滴小小的幸福灌溉不可
十八年一次　决定去死或决定忘记

一个岛突出海面上一座阳台
一个仪式　十八年后晃着一只柠檬的

3 Anniversary, 9th October 1989

life's decisions   sometimes too hard sometimes too easy
the plank walls of this rented room are gloomy and dark
like a negative that has developed many images
fixative soaking though into a wedding
you and I   clothes as clean as a hotel bed sheet
you have newly washed and starched
Minford   Duncan   Stuart
three friends bringing champagne and flowers
that weird October spring   setting alight
the little mushroom-shaped trees across the road
this was Auckland   the lawns inlaid with life
carefully written down in the witness column
the bluest sea in the world

the faces of all the relatives who weren't at the wedding
were all there   the beach dyed black with volcanic ash
hung with a row of huge and coldly colourful irises
waiting here earlier   the long downhill path seemed an injection of
history   injecting us with the upside-down season
the pale pink that makes paint on an old house peel
chasing a tent in a storm   locked in white clouds
locked by the sky's miles per hour inside the window frame

our dizziness too grew into an incident
just as love overflowed the cliffs of each night
a look over the shoulder   pushing our endlessly unfinished
leap in the air   on this date
the ghostly bracken is fresh, tender, fatly green
must be watered with two drops of tiny happiness
once every eighteen years   decide to die or decide to forget

an island sticking out from a balcony on the sea
a ceremony   eighteen years later dazzling in lemon

金色　日子既没变大也没变小
却一一历数我们的肉的破碎海岸
诗再写也碰不到一把指缝间漏下的
蓝色沙子　你藏进雪白的兰花
修饰患难的灿烂的脖子　岁月
像件赠给我们自己的礼物
珍藏得够深　老房子拆除时咳出一口尘土
红色独木舟瞪着珍珠母眼珠出海
被雕刻成的正是被毁灭成的样子

gold   the days have grown neither large nor small
yet to count every broken seashore of our flesh piece by piece
and poems written again can't yet collide with the blue sand
dribbling through the fingers   you hide in snow-white orchids
modifying a neck magnificent in adversity   years
like presents we give ourselves
hoarded deep enough   the old house coughs a mouthful of dust as it's
                                                    demolished
the red canoe stares with abalone pupils as it sets sail
what it's carved into is the shape it's destroyed into

4 流去——写在水上的字

河的书　　总在撕掉血淋淋的一页
滑铁卢桥牵着灯光的彗尾
而你眼中渗出的黑暗
像石块　　锚在水下
看城市被潮涨潮落磨灭

看一滴孤独压弯光年的蛛网
我的脸也从你眼中渗出
一道抬高博物馆的波浪
自由地　　滚滚地　　吞咽更多离别
无论是水或是血

4 Floating away – Written on water

the book of the river   always tearing up a blood-drenched page
Waterloo Bridge dragging its comet-tail of lights
and darkness leaking from your eyes
like rocks   anchored underwater
watching how the city is erased by ebb and flow of the tides

watching a drop of loneliness buckle a web of light-years
my face leaks out from your eyes too
a wave that lifts museums high
freely   surgingly   swallowing more farewells
whether of water or blood

5 大海，安魂曲，首次，也是再次

船头慢吞吞压进一片蓝　这一瞬
有什么永远碎了　海鸥的眼神
既美丽又狂暴　扑向水平线的船舷
带路的是一只龙骨下悠游的小海豚
穿透了什么　比阳光油漆的皮肤更激烈
像背上黑亮喷气的小圆孔一样深
俯瞰着我们模仿鳍挥动的胳膊
和　刚刚抹平一个浪的内心

最彻底的粉碎是看不见的　水滴
把一双手静静折断　蓝的隐喻
既给灵魂又给大海　蘸一下就斑斑龟裂
抽出　来不及退去的阴影就学着作曲
我们的两只音符被一条水线串着
两次演奏　使每个距离偷偷加倍
剥开海的刺　一枚仙人掌果红如血缘的
肉　让我们牙床上溅满了彼此

我们已驶过了多少海洋啊　多少光
保持着年幼　磨快折刀似的翅膀
一张床拖着航迹　航行到我们的
成熟里　家　从这个词望去海水最苍茫
潮汐的桌子上摆满疑问　再推迟
一行诗句就是一块浮石　远方
好近啊　我们能感到它在怀抱里孵化
爱　从这个词想象涛声拍打的形象

只两个人　加一个星空　别无所求
只一天　一个拧亮又熄灭的节奏
把船舷边画下水痕的世界冲刷而去
你我的嘴唇安置什么也不遗漏的结构
完美的漩涡　只待剑鱼深长的一吻
黎明像个最后剩下的　最炫目的理由
值得交换我脸颊上浅浅的凹陷
当你醒了　在那儿停泊你的额头

126

5 Ocean, requiem, the first time and once more

sluggishly the boat's prow presses into blue   in these seconds
something is broken forever   the look in the seagulls' eyes
is beautiful and violent   bends toward the gunwale's horizons
the leisurely dolphins that lead the way   swimming under our keel
have penetrated something   sharper than sunlight-painted skins
deep as their little black shining blowholes
looking down over them our arms wave in imitation of fins
and   our hearts have just smoothed out the breaking waves

the most drastic shattering can't be seen   drops of water
gently break two hands   blue metaphor
is for the soul and for the sea   dip in and crack like stained turtle-shell
pull out   shadow too late to retreat learns to be a composer
our two notes are linked by a water-line
twice performed   making every distance stealthily double
the splinter that peels the sea   the meat of cactus-fruit red as
blood ties   has spattered our gums with one another

oh we have sailed across so many oceans   so much lustre
keeping young   whetted penknives like wings
a bed dragging the boat's trace   sailing into our
maturity   home   looking out from this word the sea is vaster
doubts spread over the table-top of tides   once again defer
a line of verse and then it's a pumice stone   farther
oh, very near   we can feel it hatch in our inner being
love   from this word we conjure up the image pounded out by the waves' roar

only two people   plus a starry sky   seeking no less
only one day   a rhythm squeezed bright then quenched
scours away the gunwales' world of painted waterlines
our lips, yours and mine, fix a structure where nothing is passed over
a perfect vortex   only awaiting a swordfish's long and deep kiss
dawn like the last left-over   most blinding reason worth
swapping for the shallow hollows on my cheeks
as you awake   there is your forehead's berth

当时间　这音乐的语法　不谈论终点
却以每个疯狂的一生照耀那终点
插在一个余温袅袅的洞穴里赴死
不是无限　平庸的下午一阵突袭的孤单
虚拟着无限　我们静静对坐的房间
淋着比无限更远的细雨　聆听
海浪破译的电报声　两颗心依然惊讶
我们的鲜艳　尽管日子哑口无言

于是安魂曲和大海呈现同一种美
一首爱情诗等来首次　抖动的蓝轮回
无数次　每次一个不堪忍受的世界
精雕细刻一枝向你擎出的凤尾
沙滩上无数条投奔浪花的路
用我们那条　指挥璀璨的乐队
给你一个阳光修剪的腰身的调性
你拧着湿淋淋头发里的海水

修复我的视觉　哦　活过
就是铺开自己这张血肉的乐谱
写下古老的荡漾　抚摸
从一双眼睛倾入另一双眼睛的万顷碧波
雪亮　等于皮肤下的暗夜
巨鲸的残骸像盏苍白的灯幽幽垂落
我们的美一如我们的碎　持在谁手上
云来了　笔尖沙沙风暴的杰作

把你的手放进我手中　一个旅程
背诵一次就再经历一次　诗这样生成
水薄荷的纤维一百万年只编织一次
绿绿你我　像个对惨痛诗意的约定
学会爱就是学会在一条街的甲板上稳住
学会死　虚无有多深温柔有多深　幸福
生成　你掌心里的热已渗透我的骨髓
两只水鸟翅尖一碰　停下我们的造形

as time   this music's grammar   doesn't discuss endings
but illuminates that ending with every life of madness
going to die stuck in a cave where warmth lingers
is not infinity   on a commonplace afternoon a surprise attack of loneliness
pretends infinity   the room where we sit quietly facing each other
drips with a fine drizzle farther away than infinity   listen closely to
the telegram the waves decode   two hearts surprised still
by how colourful we are   even though the days are speechless

so they seem identically beautiful, the ocean and the requiem
a love poem waits for the first time   trembling blue recurs
times without number   each time an unendurable world
holds a carefully-carved phoenix-tail fern toward you
beach roads without number run to seek refuge in the spume
use the one we have   to conduct a dazzling orchestra
giving you the tonality of a sun-trimmed waistline
you're wringing seawater from your dripping hair

restore my vision   oh   to have lived
is to spread out the score of your own flesh and blood
write down the ancient undulations   fondle
the immensity of blue waves from where one pair of eyes falls into another
snow-bright   equal to the dark night below the skin
the huge whale's bones like pale lamps faintly tumble
our beauty is like our brokenness   held in whose hand
come the clouds   the masterpiece of the storm in pen point scribble

put your hand in mine   an itinerary
memorised once then experienced once more   so a poem is born
in a million years watermint's fibres have only once woven
so green you and so green me   appointing a bitter poetic
learning to love is learning how to stand steady on the street's deck
learning to die   nothingness how deep gentleness how deep   so delight
is born   the heat in your palm has seeped into my marrow
once two water birds' wingtips collide   it brings our created images to a halt

水薄荷叙事诗（三）

——历史哀歌

WATERMINT NARRATIVE 3

History Elegy

我的历史场景之一：

屈原，楚顷襄王十五年

一道水的明亮皱褶里叠印他和你的
脚步　一道光检测着祖屋的老
像被判决终身奄奄一息的火塘
暮色也是件没有时态的作品
把他的高冠　长剑　兰蕙　华章
玉佩之叮当　埋进你枕着的泥岸
小时候意味着几千年？一排浪牵动
江心的大轮船　汽笛声中等待之诗
早成相思之诗　水浸浸的距离
忘了也在一只明月灯笼的吟咏下
记住　祖屋旁的韵脚清自清浊自浊
相思自是一种交给毁灭攥紧的形式
哦　大夫　一间筑在水中的斗室
小自小　大自大　足够无尽徘徊

他和你都不会惊奇　"南州之美莫如澧"
一条河也有它独一无二的体味儿
像美人　辗转身边如一根熏衣的香草
断也是决绝的　一个投水的姿势
令一段江面腰肢挺起　一枚玉玦
又一枚玉玦　追着水鸟掷入江风
多好闻啊　一天天把你怀大的鱼腥
从一千条河中选出这一条　呛炸

Qu Yuan, 283 BC, the 15th year of King Qingxiang of Chu[26]

in the bright wrinkle of a stretch of water the double exposure of his and your
footsteps   a shaft of light tests the age of the ancestral hall
like the fire pit sentenced to a single lifelong last gasp
twilight is a tenseless opus too
burying   his mitre   scimitar   orchids   gorgeous poems
tinkling of jade pendants   buried in the muddy shore that pillowed you
does childhood imply millennia?   a row of waves drags at
the steamer in the heart of the river   poems of waiting in its steam whistle
became poems of lovesickness long ago   the drenched distance
forgotten also under a moon-lantern's recitation
remembers   rhyme-words by the ancestral hall, turbid or clear in themselves
lovesickness itself a form gripped by ruin
oh   Master   a cell built in water
small in itself   large in itself   enough for endless pacing

he and you can both wonder   *of Southland's beauties none compares to the*
River Li

a river has it own unique body-odour too
like a beautiful woman   turning beside you like a sprig of lavender
any rejection must be resolute   the gesture of jumping into the water
straightens the river's back   a jade belt-ring
another jade belt-ring   thrown into the river breeze after the water birds
oh so sweet the smell   the rank stench that made you day by day more gravid
choose this river out of a thousand rivers   explosive choking

---

26. Qu Yuan (*fl.* 4th-3rd century BC), the earliest named poet in the Chinese
tradition, took his life in protest at his sovereign's neglect: the annual Dragon
Boat Festival commemorates his death. (NB: *Qu* is pronounced *chü*, like French
tu; *Chu* has the rounded vowel of English *choo-choo*.) See David Hawkes, *The
Songs of the South: An Anthology of Ancient Chinese Poems by Qu Yuan and Other
Poets* (Penguin Books, 1985) ISBN 0-14-044375-4

大夫的肺　郢已破　东门已芜
妃子已荡靛绿的涟漪　该写的句子呢
落一场非湖非海锁入流向的大雪
女孩的身体鲜艳迎迓一首诗的冒犯
女孩默想　踢过的浪多远了　多老了
水声汩汩　屋顶　墙缝渗漏的黑
招认　当苦苦相思像个虚构横渡不了
美人都不耐烦自己的美丽

五十二岁时我重读被你拣回的
二十九岁　自恋像只萤火虫
睡着的火山怀着暗红的年号
——"树根缓慢地扎进心里"
——"它学会对自己无情"
过盛的时间清澈过滤河底不流的疑问
水之老筛掉大夫春夜的恼怒
再读　我们的才华连自戕都不会
只能忍住霉烂椽子上你的乡音
滴进我的　递增一只漩涡的聋哑
你的祖屋变卖给鹭鸶　吊着兽性的脚
啄起白白的尸体　我们连死亡都用尽了
何况相思　玩过的浪滚动成远山
何况诀别的空书从不留下任何名字
哪怕叫澧水　模拟无人的温柔
从一千个侧面教给耳朵干渴的诗意

of the Master's lungs   Chu's capital in ruin   East Gate overgrown
concubines a ripple in the *Indigo Record*   and the lines that should have
                                                    been written?
they fell into a snowstorm locked into a current neither lake nor sea
young girls' bodies gaudily greet a poem's affront
girls' musing   the kicked-at waves how far away now   how old
the gurgling waters   darkness that leaks through cracks in wall and roof
confess   in a lovesickness bitter as fiction no one could swim over
all lovely women are impatient with their beauty

at fifty-two I read again the age of twenty-nine you chose to
retrieve   self-love like a firefly
a sleeping volcano cherishing a crimson reign-title
    tree roots unhurriedly pierced his heart
    it learns to be merciless to itself
too-thriving time's limpidity filters the unflowing riverbed's suspicion
the water's old sieve sheds the Master's anger on that spring night
re-reading   our talent doesn't even know how to commit suicide
can only endure your country accent on mouldy rafters
dripping into mine   increasing a vortex's deaf-muteness
your ancestral hall has been sold off to egrets   hung with beast's paws
pecking pale white corpses   we have even used up death
let alone lovesickness   the waves we played in billow into far-off mountains
let alone empty books of condolence where no name will ever be left
even calling it the Li River   copying a non-personal tenderness
from a thousand sides teaching the ear a dry and desiccated poetics

巴勃罗·卡萨尔斯，一九五五年五月十五日

纪念馆的小门隐在旅客咨询处后面
关掉节目单的五颜六色
一头老象　　突兀在房间里
灰暗多皱地摆动

一根老弦把灰暗多皱的鼻子探入
下一小节　　猛汲会痉挛的水
音乐　　他的胸腔把惊飞的时代
改编成徐徐叹出的哼声

玻璃橱柜中石膏的五指
还领奏着大海　　一付小圆花镜
还在摘下脸上悲苦的玫瑰窗
一只旧皮箱还在朝一切方向上路

除了故乡那个方向　　一山之隔
便是虚无　　一只冷血的音叉校对他
蜇入租来的家就一点点融入
朋友们的亡灵　　一块老茧

打磨决定沉默的十八年
空白的早晨层层脱皮成一首组曲
街道等在雨中　　练习屏住呼吸
他的宁静无限缩小了独裁者

他的缺席把一张琴变得庞大
在一个有名有姓的回绝里
删去不值得聆听的
岁月般琐碎的

SCENES FROM MY HISTORY 2

Pablo Casals, 15th May 1955

the little door of the Memorial Hall hidden behind Tourist Information
shuts off the programme's many colours
an old elephant   pushes out into the room
a dark grey wrinkled lurching

an old cello string explores a dark-grey wrinkled nose
in the next measure   violently draws water music
that will spasm   his chest rearranges an era startled into flight
into the drone of a gentle sigh

the five plaster fingers in the glass display case
still conduct an ocean   little round long-sighted spectacles
still take grief's rose-window off his face
an old leather suitcase still setting off in all directions

except for the direction of home   the other side of the mountains
is nothingness   a cold-blooded tuning fork calibrates him
walking into a rented house then slowly melting into
the ghosts of friends   an old cocoon

eighteen years burnishing the decision to be silent
blank mornings flayed layer by layer into a dance suite
streets waiting in the rain   practised holding their breath
as his silence perpetually shrank the dictator

his absence made a cello enormous
in a named refusal
it expunged what's not worth listening to
trivia like years

移开自己多余的名字
他的烟斗　他的狗　慢慢转过街角
都是深度节拍器　他的老年
（一如所有老年）　没有渺小的叙事

那双手令天空震动地闲着
知道　死亡更近
耽溺在不演奏时更怕人的柔情里
知道纪念馆的幽暗渗出血丝

（一声录音里响了半个世纪的咳嗽
咳出这首诗　注册我的网站被祖国
绞杀的一刻　噩耗
把我逐出听众的位置）

大洋环流的教堂里一把木椅子
没搅碎沉默　只铆定沉默
历史有个缓缓坐下去的重量
触弦的是　重申不

在我诞生第八十三天
葡萄园的绿色乐谱叮咛一个婴儿
诗是什么　储存了十八岁的无声后
大提琴地狱般的开口意味着什么

此外　音乐呢
音乐在纪念馆的石板地上洒水
罩着我们的爱的荫凉　心
追上听清惨痛的至少的幸福

removing his surplus name
his pipe   his dog   slowly turning the street corner
all one metronome of depth   his years of old age
(like all years of old age)   there is no smaller narrative

the resting of those hands that once shook the sky
knew   death was nearer
when he lost himself in not playing a more terrifying sympathy
he knew the streaks of blood seeping from the Memorial Hall's darkness

(the recording replays half a century of coughs
coughs up this poem   the moment registering my website
was strangled by my motherland   the worst of news
drove me from my seat in the audience)

a wooden chair in a church hall of circumfluent oceans
shattered no silence   just fixed silence down
history has a weight that sits slowly down
YES touching a string   reaffirms NO

when I had been eighty-three days born
the vineyard's green score cautioned the infant
what poetry is   with eighteen years of silence in stock
a cello speaking in the voice of hell means what?

this apart   what is music now?
music splashed on the flagstones of the Memorial Hall
covers the cool shade of our love   the pursuing heart
hears with clarity the smallest excruciating happiness

我的历史场景之三：

严文井，二零零五年七月二十日

（天堂的半途——）

我总是赶不上一场葬礼

甚至猫咪欢欢也比我快
一座正午暴晒的阳台也比我快
等着烫死的方便面已吃够了沙尘暴

围棋盘上的残局蚕食这七月
他在路上　　天堂在不远不近的地方

只是他的死给小屋唤来造访者
只是　　最后十年清冷反锁的
私酿的孤寂　　再也不可造访
匆忙的人生理解不了　　两根手指微微
抖动　　黑白棋子间历史倏然转折
他的沉思夹着自己的落点
而我诡谲地想象一块遗照上的玻璃
把凛冽的幽默都焐热了
十年前一串从窗口扔下来的钥匙
拧开悔恨　　不接住就好了
一条拖着脚挪向小饭馆的路
永远走不到

或许能刹住头脑中嗡嗡轰鸣的海啸
"最后一次！"

　　　　　但他目光一闪
"没有开始哪儿来最后？"
天堂列车上缀满蜡制的猫眼

Yan Wenjing, 20th July 2005 [27]

(Halfway to Heaven)

I'm never in time for a funeral

even his kitty Huanhuan is quicker than me
a balcony basking in the noonday sun is quicker than me too
pot noodles waiting to be scalded to death have eaten their fill of the sandstorm

the endgame on the chessboard nibbles at this July
he was on the way   heaven a place neither near nor far

only his death summoned visitors to the little room
only   the final decades of chill locked-in
bootleg loneliness   could never again visit
hurrying Life couldn't understand   two fingers feebly
trembling   history abruptly transiting between black chessmen and white
his pondering as he set out where he'd touch down
and me craftily imagining the glass on the funeral photo
warming a bitter cold humour
a bunch of keys thrown through a window ten years ago
to open deep regret   better never to have caught them
the road where he dragged his feet to the little restaurant
will never arrive

can maybe brake the tsunami's buzzing roar in the brain
'last time!'

    but in his flashing eyes
'without a beginning, how do we reach the end?'
the train to heaven is all studded with waxen cat's eyes

---

27. Yan Wenjing (1915-2005), popular children's author, born in Hubei.

141

欢欢瞳孔中冷凝的荧火
像条蜡制轨道承运少年的云
某个湖北孩子的顽皮
切开故事中一块蜡的人格
影子返身割下难忍的生命
九十年　他写一本书　而拖欠交稿的
三个月　像童声嘹亮的缺口
广场上盆栽的笑是编号的
背诵的节日袅袅舔向未来
某种人性的肺气肿
发育成半夜呛醒他的暴戾目的
某个想象力的渺小谎言
把别人的脸掀开一点　借着误解
把公式推开　天堂无限远
半途娇纵如老年的色情
直到什么都不发生的日子
比哪本书都说出更多
他额头的光辐射烧融那么多童年
最后一场核爆　冗长的世纪
精练成一个下午

红庙北里　女儿一星期来一次
拿报纸　送食品　铁窗框间偷渡阳光
欢欢的叫声菩萨般圆满

一本弃置到远远内心里的旧棋谱
弃置不配镌刻历史的国度
天空喘息　小屋里继续飘落的灰
静悄悄混合了他的灰

托梦的湖北口音仍在攀升的半途？
即将完成的视线在夷平楼群的半途？
天堂有鸟鸣　我赶不上葬礼
同样　赶不上人生

fluorescent condensation in Huanhuan's pupils
like a waxen railway carrying the clouds of youth
the naughtiness of some Hubei kid
cuts through the wax personalities of storybook characters
shadows turn about to amputate an intolerable life
at ninety   he wrote a book   and was three months late
submitting it   a gap resounding as a child's voice
bonsai smiles all numbered in the square
festivals of recitation kink and lap at the future
emphysema of some kind of humanity
develops into a fierce intent that chokes him awake at night
petty lies of some imagination
open other people's faces a little   borrow misunderstandings
to reject a formula   heaven is infinitely far away
halfway pampering is like sex in old age
until the days when nothing happens
say more than any book
light rays from his brow evaporated so many childhoods
the final atomic explosion   a tedious century
distilled into one afternoon

at Hongmiao Beili   a daughter comes once a week
brings newspapers   presents   sneaks sunshine through the steel window frame
Huanhuan's miaow is bodhisattva-perfect

an old chess manual discarded deep in the innermost heart
to discard a nation unqualified for engraving our history
sky wheezes   ash falls on through the little room
quietly mingles with his ashes

is the Hubei accent that comes in dreams still climbing halfway?
is the soon-completed vision halfway to the flattened tower blocks?
there's birdsong in heaven   I'm late for the funeral
in the same way   I'm late for life

鱼玄机，唐懿宗八年

（一首和诗）

断头的故事绵延成欧洲的雨
断裂声打在雨伞上　不像哀泣
倒像会漫步的醉　满天纺着细丝
一条石子路铺进两场远走高飞
　　　一杯酒　浇向她的死和你的歌
　　　两绺冲淡　合唱的血色

为什么我猜她的枷衣准淋得精湿
一如你　随风吹洒的淙淙响的句子
为什么我猜一颗硕大的水滴
裹住上千年　你们的头巾兜紧药味？
　　　我的臂弯里一张最娇艳的脸
　　　猛地挣出大海幽闭的房间

写她的死　你是否分担那个死期？
一次处决　回旋成织锦的回文诗
青山如刃　雪亮地掠过脖子
刽子手们跨时空的亲昵
　　　扼住你们身上最细最纤弱之处
　　　才华和多情　自古犯了众怒

这就是罪　毁掉一具具绝美的躯体
剥啊　剥出无所谓男女的辞
和眼泪　新年早上一阵孤独突袭
蓝天　卸妆吧　泻下杀伤力
　　　她粘粘猩红的长发还挽在脑后
　　　打滚　像只掰开的石榴

144

Yu Xuanji,[28] 8th year of Emperor Tang Yizong (AD 841)

(Response Poem)[29]

a story of beheading extends into in the European rain
crackling on umbrellas   unlike bitter tears
it reflects a wandering drunk   all the sky spins silk fine
a flagstone road unfolds two ways to run far away
         poured on her death and your song   a glass of wine
         two streaks of diluted   blood-coloured refrain

why do I guess her yoke and her dress were utterly sodden
like you   gurgling lines scattered by the squall
why do I guess an immense drop of water
wraps a millennia and more   are herbal cures all bound tight in your shawl?
         in the crook of my arm the daintiest face
         wildly struggles out from a sea of confinement

write her death   do you also share responsibility for her last hour?
once executed   wheeling into a palindrome of brocade
green mountains like blades   flitting snow-bright across her nape
the executioner's relatives who leap over time and space
         grab the most slim and fragile parts of your bodies
         talent and passion   have always met with public rage

and this is the crime   one after another the loveliest bodies are destroyed
oh peel away   flay the indifferently masculine or feminine words
and tears   on New Year morning an ambush of solitude
blue skies   make-up off   her lethality bled out
         long sticky scarlet hair still coiled behind her head
         it rolls about   like a split pomegranate

---

28. Yu Xuanji (*fl.* 9th century), poet, possibly rejected Imperial concubine and/or Taoist recluse, who may have been executed for murdering a servant.
    29. Or echo poem: that is, a poem made in response to one of Yu Xuanji's, using the same metre as hers.

咬着泥土　让桃花片片对你耳语
不必怨　也别怕爱　只要一次
会心地对视　香妃墓上沙尘亮丽
如镜　倒映千年间幻化的姐妹
　　　彼此的名字像散落风中的狂想
　　　爱得久一点　无论爱刺痛或一缕余香

小城瓦莱赛的雨生不逢时
我走　像只生不逢地的低飞的燕子
穿过你们　书写的鱼跳舞的鱼
好香　破网而出的玄机
　　　揪心的悲欢味儿　穷尽
　　　照片上继续灿烂下去的残忍

为什么我猜最解渴的仍是时间这池
浅浅的水？当死亡不是畏惧　是事实
活过　爱过　写过　断头仅标志
盛开　我的脚步既向东又向西
　　　追上双倍的不可能
　　　笑意　才钉进一双最忧郁的眼睛

她的或你的？唐朝是件缥缈的羽衣
所有凌波步都向一个熟识的身影折回
死一次　碎玉打翻青羊宫的荷叶
生无数次　我们不开灯的房间里
　　　掌心疼得夺目　血迹
　　　深陷成刀尖下艳丽的纯诗

146

biting the mud   makes each peach blossom whisper no blame
to you   and don't be afraid to love   if only one time
see eye to understanding eye   the dust bright on the Imperial Concubine's
                                                                    tomb
as a mirror   reflects sisters transforming in a millennium
        their names like a fantasy dispersing in the storm
        loving longer   to love regardless of lingering perfume or stabbing pain

in the little town of Varese the rain was born at the wrong time
I stride   like a low-skimming swallow born in the wrong spot
through all of you   book-written fish dancing fish
the mystery that broke the net escaping   how sweet
        the heartrending taste of joy and sorrow   reaches the limit
        of the brutality shining on in the snapshot

why do I guess that of all things the most thirst-quenching
is still time's shallow water?   as death is not dread   but reality
to have lived   to have loved   to have written   a merely symbolic beheading
opens in bloom   my steps move both east and west
        pursuing a doubled impossibility
        only then can a smiling face   nail down the saddest eyes

hers or mine?   the Tang era is a barely-visible feather cape
each walk on water turns back toward a well-known shade
die once   in Grey Goat Palace lotus leaves toppled by broken jade
are born times without number   in rooms where we don't turn on the light
        palms in blinding pain   bloodstain
        dazzlingly pure poetry trapped under the blade

修昔底德斯，当他徘徊在锡拉库札

海浪不骗人　　它的雅典口音
缠着死者坟上一枝枝断桨
溺爱的蓝继续划动
阳光锈住了　　眼眶的无花果
空着　　那挡在回家路上的半岛
不存在　　我们来这里
只为尝尝自己肉里渗出的咸
大理石渗出雪白的诅咒
证实　　倾圮不分地点
废墟的侧面支离破碎
密密刻满字母　　俯冲如
一只只从他掌中凶猛攫食的海鸥
水平线的叫声又冷又亮
那刺穿青铜盾牌的水
结晶在死者焦渴的嘴边
像个妄想中的胜利
修昔底德斯　　来此寻访亡灵的
袍子里的风鼓动奖给一切诗人的
叛国罪　　不认识的词
"公元前"　　踩响地雷
可乐瓶　　碎电脑　　灵柩
跨着正步　　蒙在国旗下
摆进翱翔的机器
他的仪仗队是个干裂的港口
柱廊和蜥蜴　　相同的两栖类
听见心里一片海日日退去
舔不到脚趾的灿烂波浪　　拉开
旷野　　撕散的棉桃像两行足迹
我们的远征总背对海
像一场和自己无休止的争论
"他们蹂躏了那地方，就回去了"
史书这样写我们死亡的意义

Thucydides, hesitating before Syracuse

a wave doesn't cheat   its Athenian accent
entangles every broken oar on the graves of the dead
pampered blue paddles on
sunlight has rusted   the figs of the eye sockets
emptying   the peninsula that blocks the road home
non-existent   we came here
just to taste the salt that oozes from our flesh
marble oozes snow-white curses
confirms   collapse is no respecter of places
ruin's profile is chaotic fragments
densely carved with letters   swooping like
all the greedy seagulls snatching food from his hand
cries from the horizon are cold and bright
water that pierced bronze shields
crystallised on the parched lips of the dead
like a victory without hope
Thucydides   came here to seek the departed
wind in his tunic inciting the treason awarded
to all poets   the unknown words
Before Christ   set off landmines
coke bottles   broken computers   coffins
goose-stepping   under cover of the nation's flag
positioned in hovering machines
his guard of honour is a harbour cracked by drought
colonnades and lizards   identically amphibian
hear the sea in the heart retreat day by day
magnificent waves that can't lap at his toe   drag open
a wilderness   spilt cotton like two rows of footprints
our expedition always with our backs to the sea
like the never-ending debate with ourselves
they laid that place waste, and turned back
so history books write the meaning of our death

奇形怪状的海岸上
仙人掌果坠着血红的乳头
束着腰的胡桃树下
毁灭背对每一个故乡
"他们蹂躏了那地方，就回去了"
简洁的句子拖着地中海
刮平的　神谕摸不到的海底
罗马　拿破仑　不列颠
一捧捧火山灰庞然倒扣下
瞎眼的鹰扛着今天的帝国
但我们是回不去的
乌有的意义是回不去的
我们的家埋在别人粉碎的家里
修昔底德斯精致研究
一朵浪花跌落的绝对性
我们的蹂躏　唯一赢得了
一声枪击的沉闷感谢
一片走投无路的摇落的松荫
对每只耳朵都是外语
没人听懂时只对自己说
活人听不见就对死人说
修昔底德斯　本身是亡灵
沿着希腊的溃败　布置
一座两边都是海的高耸的石门
湛蓝耀眼的穿越
等于同一场沉没
回家的路本不存在
因为大海那边本没有家
因为我们比大海更空旷
唯有厌倦这唯一一边
厌倦于自己的分裂
和在潮水上记录分裂的努力
一个吹散云朵的深长叹息
震荡肺腑　伯罗奔尼撒不在
纽约　伊拉克不在
未来尸首预约的手术

on a bizarrely-shaped seashore
cactus fruit's blood-red nipples fall
under cinched walnut trees
destruction stands with its back to every hometown
they laid that place waste, and turned back
terse sentences pull out the Mediterranean's
seabed   scraped clean   unreachable by oracles
Rome   Napoleon   Britain
yet each handful of volcanic ash is hugely fastened
blind eagles shoulder today's empires
but we cannot turn back
illusory meanings cannot turn back
our home is buried in a home someone else smashed
Thucydides researches in fine detail
the absoluteness of the falling spume
our laying waste   only won
the glum thanks of a gunfight
a dead-end in the shade of swaying pines
it's all foreign language to each ear
when no one understands   speak only to yourself
if the living can't hear   speak to the dead
Thucydides   a departed soul himself
trails Greece's crushing defeats   sets
a towering stone gate with the sea on both sides
a crossing dazzled by bright blue
equal to an identical sinking
a road home originally non-existent
because there is no home on the other side of the ocean
because we are vaster than an ocean
the one and only side is weariness
wearied by its own splitting
and the effort of recording the split on the tidewater
a long deep sigh that blows the clouds away
shaking our liver and lights   the Peloponnese is not there
New York   Iraq   not there
operations booked by future corpses

151

溅起堆堆疯狂演讲的泡沫
早缝合了　树叶翻开惨白的底牌
我们的鱼骨斜插在书里
盯着看　四周粗硬的沙粒
涌出腐蚀的颜色
修昔底德斯抚摸一个淤血的字
大海这块痂　抚摸过
被蹂躏的人的可能性
回不去时　回到
一枝戳疼天空的断桨
第一眼就被蓝的浓度宠坏了
把噩耗研磨得更细些
写出历史

splatter the piled-high froth of all the speeches
long ago sewed up   the deathly pale cards the leaves turn over
our fish bones are stuck askew in the books
staring at   coarse sand all around us
gushing out corrupted colour
Thucydides fondles a blood-deposited word
the scab of the sea   has fondled
the possibility of people laid waste
when they can't turn back   turning back to
a broken oar stabbing at the sky
the first eye spoiled by the density of blue
meticulously polishes the worst possible news
writes out history

克丽斯塔·沃尔芙，一九九二年

柏林的满月复活一次背叛

她写过那房子　此刻房子走出房子
她写过那街道　此刻街道漂流出街道
她写过的大海抬高剖腹产的床

卡珊德拉　美狄亚　克丽斯塔
血淋淋押韵

谁给阴影一个轮廓不得不血淋淋

像月光的视力　刨出
女人薄薄掩埋的银白骸骨
铺路石透明分裂的眸子
盯着墙的平行线　迈锡尼　科林斯　北京
满是弹洞　而卵巢像靶心
她在一座座城市的碎玻璃上赤脚起舞

情人们睡进冰川的怀抱
跟着步伐娇小的作品移动

刺绣现在　肉吱嘎作响的擦痕
编织一次褪色　检查站的
探照灯像女巫爆炸　满月鸡尾斑斓
被过去辞退才双倍呕出现在

她写不洁　剧毒　精确之美

Christa Wolf,[30] 1992

the Berlin full moon revives a betrayal

she had written that house   now the room left the house
she had written that street   now the street drifted out of the street
the ocean she written lifted the caesarean bed high

Cassandra   Medea   Christa
a rhyme dripping with blood

whoever delineates shadows has no choice but to drip with blood

like moonlight's vision   digging up
silvery white bones of a woman in a shallow grave
flagstones' eye-pupils split by transparency
staring at the wall's parallel lines   Mycenae   Corinth   Beijing
riddled with bullet holes   and ovaries like bulls-eyes
barefoot she danced on the shattered glass of every city

lovers sleep into the glacier's embrace
move in step with their works' dainty opus

to embroider the now   striations of flesh crunching
to weave only once a fade hue   the checkpoint's
searchlights like witches exploding   the full moon cocktail glorious
dismissed by the past it doubly spews out the now

she writes filth   hypertoxic   a precise beauty

---

30. Christa Wolf (1929-2011), East German author and critic.

一把铁椅子又冷又硬硌疼室内
一声轻轻甚至刻意温柔的"说吧"
一颗心陡然沉下去的空
娇小的"完了"受限于重量的物理学
呼喊从拢在嘴边的手指间泄漏
勃兰登堡门前　　那女孩儿
听觉的金羊毛正兑换成
一簇锈迹斑斑的青铜阴毛

她的写　　写下我们之间银波粼粼
一个填满征兆的黑海

背叛　　每个对她背过身去的墙角
出卖　　镂在抿紧唇线上的冷笑
偿还　　月光的债　　越皎洁欠下越多的债

克丽斯塔　　美狄亚　　卡珊德拉

背叛不值得的活
同时背叛不值得的死

房子走出房子　　水底废墟嶙峋
街道漂流出街道　　水波复制着耻辱
自行车蒙着林荫上演一部歌剧
徐徐捕杀自己孩子的夜晚
从柏林远行　　抵达
只有女人试着薄薄掩埋的
血污之美　　急促之美

无数满月辞一样准时升起
肯定最初一轮艳冶的构思
爱上还能继续涨潮的疼
活　　在　　死亡深深的照耀中

an iron chair both cold and hard presses painfully on the room's interior
a soft and even scrupulously gentle 'so speak then'
a void the heart suddenly falls into
a dainty   'it's over'   restricted by a weight's physics
shouts leak from between fingers that closed the mouth
in front of the Brandenburg Gate   that girl
hearing's golden fleece exchanged for
a bush of bronze pubic hair streaked with rust

what she wrote   wrote down the clarity of the silver waves between us
a black sea crammed with portents

betrayal   every corner that turned its back on her
sell-out   every sneer engraved on pursed lips
pay-back   moonlight's debt   the more it's owed the brighter

Christa   Medea   Cassandra

betraying a life not worth living
while betraying a death not worth dying

the house left the house   seabed ruins craggy
the street drifted out of the street   waves imitated shame
bicycles in the forest's shade sang an opera
an evening to unhurriedly hunt and kill the children
travel far from Berlin   arrive
there is only the bloodstained beauty   the frantic beauty
of a woman trying out a shallow burial

innumerable full moons rise punctually as words
confirming the first one's gaudy scenario
falling in love and still the pain can rise to a higher tide
living   in   death's deep shine

叶芝，现在和以往，斯莱歌墓园

大海是一个诺言　至死不兑现
才一次性夺走我们的眺望
他的名字牵着约会的另一端
等了二十年的早晨　风声格外嚣张
本布尔本山的静默绷紧鬼魂的蓝
全世界的韵脚　应和一排海浪

成百万块化石贯穿一条血腥的线
我蹦着走　像被举在一滴水珠上
我的影子也像动物　爬过海岸
有小小肉体扼住呼吸的疯狂
有背着光的　陷进石缝的双眼
有个堆积的活过的形象

什么也别说　小教堂的语言
刻成孤零零的雕花柱子　月光
把嵌在厨房窗口的本布尔本山推远
山脊上一抹天青色　从他的诗行
斟入我的一瞥　用二十年变酸
一个未预期的我又已是陈酿

陈旧得能和他共坐　消磨爱尔兰
空旷得迷上一阵鸥啼的苍凉
他耳语　大海的缝合术鳞光闪闪
一次靠岸仍靠近离开的方向
当汽笛锈蚀的喉咙饮着浑浊的夏天
这个吻　有诀别味儿　溅到唇上

湿过　再醉人地被狂风吹干
他的墓碑擎着冷艳的青苔香
远景在我的呼吸间撒盐
骑马人像大海放出的白云一样
允诺　碧蓝弧面上一条宛如锁死的船
一次性完成我们的眺望

W.B. Yeats, now and in the past, a Co. Sligo cemetery

the ocean is a promise   not made good until dying
only then once-only snatches away our gaze
his name holds hands with the next part of the meeting
the morning has been waiting twenty years   the wind unusually wild
a ghost's azure by Ben Bulben's silence tautening
rhymes for all the world   echo the lines of the waves

millions of fossils scattered along a scarlet band
I bound along   as if on a dew drop rising
and my shadow like a beast   has climbed to the strand
with the mad idea that my breath chokes on tiny bodies
with eyes turned from the light   stuck in fissures of stone
with a stacked-up form that once was living

don't say any more   the little chapel's language
is carved on a solitary column   the moon's gleaming
pushes away Ben Bulben set in the kitchen window
on the ridge sky-scraping emerald   is poured into my glance
from lines of his verse   twenty years of souring
turned an unpredicted me into a vintage near maturing

mature enough to sit down with him   to idle Ireland away
vast enough to beglamour the bleakness of gulls crying
his whisper   the phosphorescence of ocean's sewn-up art gleaming
once near the shore and nearing the direction of parting
as the steam whistles' rusty throats drink stout-black summer
this kiss   taste of a last goodbye   on the lips splashing

once drenched   drunkenly blown dry again by a crazy squall
his tombstone lifts the cold beauty of lichen's smell
a vista scattered salt between my inhalations
horsemen like white clouds let loose by the oceans
promise   a seemingly locked-up boat on an arc of cobalt
ends our distant gaze once and for all

水薄荷叙事诗（四）

——故乡哀歌

WATERMINT NARRATIVE 4

Hometown Elegy

一、路

距离是我一生的诅咒
当蝉声以诵经众僧的俯仰之势远近
而鸣　环湖中路像座酷热的经堂
蒙着灰尘的绿沉沉下坠
阳光改写贝叶上烫银的文字
空间充斥汗味　自行车
悟透了终极在洋槐树下生锈
水泥小公园惆得水雾迷蒙
头顶悬着只缺席的海鸥
我穿行于红砖群岛间
一个明亮的姓氏衣着泥泞的白衣
率领满城仿古的琉璃鸱尾
蝉声的粘合剂把报亭　西瓜摊
搅进昨夜暴风雨的水洼
走三分钟就到了　三分钟后众僧
转身　吟哦另一个刺耳的无限

1 Road

all my life distance has been a curse
as far and near cicadas cry in the bent posture of scripture-chanting
monks   Lakeside Road like a sweltering scripture hall
is weighed down   the bottle green of dust and ash
sunlight revises the scalding silver scripture on the palm leaves
space clogged with the stink of sweat   bicycles
awakened to ultimate truth rust in the shade of plane trees
the little concrete park so weary it's blurred in the wet mist
an absent seagull hanging overhead
I thread my way through an archipelago of red brick
a bright surname wearing a muddy white coat
commanding a whole city of glazed retro roof-beasts
a glue of cicada cries mixes news stands   watermelon stalls
into the puddles from last night's rainstorm
three minutes' walk and you're there   after three minutes the monks
turn round   to chant another ear-piercing infinity

二、雪：另一个夏天的挽诗

与活相比　诗算什么　夏天的房间
堆满我们自己的雪　供桌似的雪山
万匹素白　无鸟的天空满目烟黑
喝　扩散肿胀噩耗的　必是一场大醉

再冷　死者也不怕了　我们携来苦酒
相拥而哭　哭出的夜在海拔上漂流
帐篷边　南十字星低低拎着冰柱
血里一滴酒精　世上一次轮回的虚无

再远　也无非消失成雪花的六棱形
千年之雪　一把抓起多少时空
裹着白绸不愿醒来　每天裹着灰烬
活算什么　梦更难忍　尽管我们殊死否认

2 Snow: dirge for another summer

compared to life   what is poetry worth   summer's chamber
full of our own heaped snow   snowy mountains like an altar
a million bolts of white silk   smoky black the birdless sky
drink   spread swollen news of the disaster   it'll have to be a binge and a half

colder now   but the dead aren't afraid   bitter wine we bring
embrace and weep   the wept-out night at sea level drifting
by the tent   the Southern Cross droops as it carries icicles
a drop of alcohol in the blood   in this world the void of once reincarnating

farther   to vanish into the snowflake's six-fold outline
a thousand years of snow   a handful clutching so much space and time
wrapped in white gauze and unwilling to wake   each day wrapped in quicklime
what is life worth   dreams more unbearable   though we desperately deny them

三、路

是否所有海滩上状如白骨的浮木
都有同一个起源？是否这条路
风中都是海盐味儿的血缘迎面拍击？
父亲的家有个涛声组成的地址
我起伏行走　　像被扔进
一粒苦杏仁咀嚼过的那么多嘴
是否这块触礁的路牌写进多少首诗
我就有多少个过去？是否一张渔网
仅仅为漏掉？祖国　发音像结石
砸着父亲每天塌陷一点的肾
是否回家意味着捡回一枚空蚌壳？
剜掉的蚌肉不对别的眼睛存在
同样不对我存在　　踩着滑板
跳过云朵的男孩子全是失重的
是否太阳也像颗慢慢深黑的老年斑？
是否思念的人就还被自己驱逐着？
还没追上父亲　耗尽毕生时机后
那一抹微笑

3 Road

doesn't all the driftwood that seems like white bones on the beach
come from the same source?   isn't this road
a sea-salt consanguinity dashing face-first into the wind?
father's home has an address made out of pounding surf
my rolling walk   is like it was thrown into
so many mouths that have been chewed by one bitter apricot kernel
isn't this reef-wrecked street name written into as many poems
as I have pasts?   isn't a fishing net
only for skipping through?   motherland   pronounced like the stone
colliding with father's kidney that sinks each day down
and doesn't going home imply bringing back an empty clam shell?
the gouged-out clam doesn't exist for other eyes
in the same way it doesn't exist for me   all boys on skateboards
who have leaped over clouds are entirely weightless
isn't the sun like slowly blackening senile plaque too?
isn't the longed-for one still expelled by their own self?
still not caught up with father   used up a lifetime of chances
that faint smile

四、移动的房间

发出脆响的钟　梦　和一袋米
某个深夜一把钥匙的开锁声
开启它的行程　爸　这房间移向你
这被召唤出的地点彩排一种更正
遗失的月色都迁入刷白的四壁
一道窗帘飘向你　幽灵般透明

幽灵般住在过去　夏天
登上一架血肉的梯子四面回顾
这被召唤出的风来自人工湖那边
这地板衬着微光缓缓远足
从过去到过去　这城市晚霞斑斓
爸　那是你　酿就时间的厚度

儿子抱来的西瓜　蓄满粉红色
儿子的目光镶在门牌上像个符咒
童年旋紧螺丝　发甜的死者
在一圈圈地平线里拧着一只线轴
细细的鼻息中一缕晨曦　胁迫
日子　悲苦和欣喜的同一结构

门小心掩上　房间栖息进诗行
香着追赶家常菜婀娜的舞姿
睡着了也觉得枕边水仙的臂膀
温软流溢　搂住一秒钟的玲珑精致
听啊　消失撒下瀑布声　冲撞
我们就显形　从头再漂泊一次

4 Shifting room

a loudly-striking clock   a dream   and a sack of rice
deep on a certain night the sound of a key unlocking
starts its journey   dad   this room shifts toward you
this summoned place rehearses a kind of correction
lost moonlights move into four whitewashed walls
a curtain flaps at you   transparent as an apparition

staying ghost-like in the past   summer
climbs a ladder of flesh to look everywhere
the summoned wind comes from the man-made lake there
the floor sets off feeble light on a leisurely outing
from past to past   this city an afterglow in every colour
dad   that's you   brewed to time's thick texture

a watermelon the son embraces   stored-up pinkish-red
son's gaze inlaid in the door's nameplate like a curse
childhood tightens the screw   the sweetening dead
in every horizon turn on an axis
the first hints of dawn in delicate breath   force
the days   the same structure of joy and regret

carefully the door is shut   the room in a line of verse roosting
tastes to catch up the dancer's home-cooked bearing
falling asleep and feeling narcissus arms by the bolster
a gentle overflow   holding a second of exquisite refinement
oh listen   vanishing discharges the sound of the waterfall   colliding
we are visible in our true form   drifting all over again from the beginning

五、路

从环湖中路到泰晤士河甚至不必过桥
一条河边搁浅的船排练完所有房子的脚本
甲板摆满绣球花　　舷梯上攀援着孩子　桨叶
一只铁蜻蜓　肥厚的五指扇着烂泥味儿的嘴巴
黄铜船钟每天两次校对擦得雪亮的时间
突然　　忘记海风的桅杆从一场暴雨收听到
隔世的温柔　　如今河在船舱形的卧室旁流过
如今橡木窗框中镶嵌的既不是岸又不是水
却有一种累　比海上厌倦了眺望的眼睛还累
搁在这儿　　呼吸比盖着青苔的小教堂更迟缓
一滩鸟粪垂直落在一行诗藏进落叶的鞋子上

5 Road

from Lakeside Road to the Thames you don't even have to cross a bridge
stranded riverbank boats have rehearsed the script of every house
decks set with hydrangeas   kids climb companionways   oar blades
an iron dragonfly   fat fingers delivering a muddy slap
twice daily brass ship's bells proofread time swabbed snow-bright
suddenly   masts that had forgotten stormy sea winds listen
to the gentleness of an earlier life now the river flows by cabin-shaped bedrooms
now what's inlaid in oak windows is neither shore nor water
but a kind of weariness   wearier than eyes exhausted by keeping watch at sea
left here   breathing more sluggishly than the little mossy chapel
a beach of bird shit falls onto a verse's shoes hidden in autumn leaves

六、京剧课

牡丹簇拥　细细的蕊上站着亭台
她的腮过渡给他　梦半红半白
他的多情婉转成她春天的歌喉
人耶鬼耶　不可能的美裳裹于世外
裳裳近了　扑鼻的粉香托起肉香
莲步　云靴　趟得连漪满池漾开
他唱　而她为每个拖长的尾音签名
人生如戏　可并非人人都演得精彩
　　　　　——父亲说

东安市场　吉祥剧院　金鱼胡同
都追着妃子　云想衣裳花想容
历史想着卸妆后的断壁残垣
她和他　美目流盼填充虚无的剧情
水袖甩着千年　谁在乎干透的名字
酒杯看不见地斟满　看不见地一饮而空
勒断的脖子悬在一场黑暗的堂会中
旋舞　真剪下的花颈迎着假的年龄
　　　　　——父亲说

世界埋伏进空气　随一声鹤唳
而显现　朝代啊　殷红惨白都是喜
一只咽喉深处逼出的唱腔逼出沧桑
永远同一个故事　永远这对男女
踩着舞台的边缘就像岁月边缘
踩着现在的刃　悬崖下大海远去
她和他俯瞰我们　非风韵到极点不可
炉火纯青啊　贯穿耳畔的沉寂
　　　　　——父亲说

6 Peking Opera lesson

peonies cluster round   on their fine stamens stand pergola and patio
her cheek transits over to him   a dream half-white half-red
his sweet tenderness becomes her springtime soprano
is't man? is't ghost?   an impossible beauty dallies with the world beyond
dalliance approaching   powder's perfume shores up the aroma of flesh
hip-swinging   high buskins   wade the riffling pool and see it overflow
he sings   and she puts her signature to each drawn-out end-rhyme
life is like theatre   but not everyone puts on a brilliant show
                                   – says Father

Eastern Peace Market   Fortuna Theatre   Goldfish Lane
all chasing the king's concubine   clouds want clothes flowers want faces
history wants broken-down relics that follow after greasepaint is gone
he and she   amorous looks and sweet ogling fill in a blank storyline
white silk sleeves have been rippling a millennium   who cares about dry names?
the shot glass is filled up all unseen   is knocked back all unseen
the snapped neck hanging from the strap in a darkened private party
pirouettes   a true cut flower has encountered an untrue maturity
                                   – says Father

a world hidden in air   materialises
with the crane's cries   oh dynasties   the crimson and the white are bliss indeed
an aria forced from deep in the throat   forces out Deep Time's metamorphoses
always the same story   always this girl and this boy
treading the margin of the stage as if it were the margin of time
treading the knife-edge of the now   the oceans below the cliff recede
she and he watch us from a great height   only extreme elegance allowed
oh how golden shines art's alembic   it pierces every silence in the ears
                                   – says Father

七、路

但酷热也在复述一种久远的亲情
街头叫卖的小贩　怀揣各自的珍宝
一场歌剧衔接得恰恰撕毁一只耳朵
水果摊老尽一颗颗甜腥的少年心
三分钟　压缩版的黄庭坚
播映还乡的跋涉　父亲演绎一个终点
一百万扇油烟四溢的厨房窗户凸向
月亮　路灯水银色的裙裾
在缝合或粉碎梦的完整性？
三分钟　走完庆幸或悔恨的族谱
热　水蛭般叮进异国情调的母语
我的拖鞋的远洋船　被万里浪打得
斑斑驳驳　在挣脱或沦入
一条最深的海沟？父亲咳嗽声的
浮标间　每一步跟上航道
怕人的吸力　这首诗和我
同样把妄想当作归来

7 Road

but the sweltering heat also retells a love from long ago
hawkers cry their wares   each holds their treasure
an opera so exactly connected shreds the ears
fruit stalls age the sweet stench of youthful hearts one by one
three minutes   the *Condensed Huang Tingjian* [31]
broadcasts the homeward trek   father deduces a destination
a million soot-spitting kitchen windows bulging out toward
the moon   street lights' quicksilver aprons
the wholeness of a stitched dream or a shattered one?
three minutes   you've walked the family tree of rejoicing or regret
hot   biting an exotic mother tongue like a leech
those ocean liners, my slippers   have been beaten black and blue
by ten-thousand league waves   freed from or fallen into
the deepest oceanic trench?   between the buoys of father's
coughs   each step catches up with the channel
a terrifying suction   this poem and I
both consider vain hope to be a return

---

31. Huang Tingjian (1045-1105), poet, painter and calligrapher, one of the Four Masters of the Song dynasty.

八、雨夜

这大雨之夜只留给世界漆黑的想象力
窗台掉进一个成千上万吨的瞬间
颤抖　谁说宇宙间水最孤独

当人还能更渺小
守着一盏灯　守着海底
一枝舍不得睡去的珊瑚

这里的大雨之夜
满地激流倒灌进耳廓　天空的
滔滔不绝有个绝不混淆的口音

一小时　在鞭打中肿胀
一棵狂风折弯的小槐树弹上浪尖
它的弹力射出它的晶体

它的乌云雕花　雕成一杯茶的纵深
听着隔壁惊醒的孩子　啼哭成
不是回忆的故乡的纵深

却更猖獗地加速　整夜
耳膜上所有失去的可能性哗哗泼下
地平线扑面而来咆哮而去

挂在更渺小的眼角上　一滴
含着你我　还在猜分别的含义
还徒劳地怕噩梦的卵再次分裂开

8 Rainy night

this night of heavy rain only leaves pitch-black imagination to the world
windowsills fallen into a thousand-ton instant
shivering   who says water is the loneliest thing in the universe?

being human can still be tinier yet
guarding a lamp   guarding the seafloor
a branch of coral that begrudges sleep

night of heavy rain here
torrents everywhere upended into the ear   the sky's
full-stream speech has an accent in no way baffling

one hour   swollen from its thrashing
a little acacia bent by mad winds bounces on the wave crests
its elasticity spurts out its crystal

its black cloud arabesque   carved into the depth of a cup of tea
hearing next door's children startled awake   weeping becomes
a depth which isn't the hometown in memory

but more furiously speeding up   all night
in the ears every lost possibility gurgles and splashes
horizons come head-on and go away roaring

hanging in the corner of a tinier eye   one drop
containing you and me   still guessing at the implications of leaving
still pointlessly afraid of the bad news egg splitting open again

九、路

爸　人生怎能有许多路？脚下
这条　或海面上秘密关掉的那些条？
　　　儿子　八十岁只留住一个黑夜
　　　磨快的锋刃足够慢慢把玩
爸　日子剪辑成一张张老照片
间隔着发黄　灯下我们翻看谁的影子？
　　　儿子　一串快门声分解你
　　　嘴里渐浓渐苦的定影液又粘合你
爸　这间小屋里你带着世界自转
按下录音键的手指　也按住
一生失恋摩擦的火花？
　　　儿子　没有什么不是快乐的知识
爸　玉琮里血丝红艳鲜嫩
活像腋窝下闪耀细细汗光的女孩儿
流浪　已给定黑暗的缘分？
　　　儿子　一条不放开你的路已
　　　够确切　够瑰丽　生命的海市蜃楼
　　　浮在没人注意的一分钟

9 Road

DAD   how can human life have many roads? this one
underfoot   or the secretly shut down ones on the sea?
       SON   the age of eighty keeps just one black night
       the whetted blade enough to play with in leisure
DAD   the days are edited into every old photo
separately yellowing   whose shadows do we flip through by lamplight?
       SON   a sequence of snapping shutters disintegrates you
       then fixative viscous and bitter in the mouth bonds you
DAD   you carry the turning world's rotation in this little room
does the finger that presses the record button   also press
the spark rubbed out by a lifetime of lost love?
       SON   there's no knowledge that isn't joyful
DAD   bloodstains scarlet and fresh in the ritual jade cylinder
the living image of girls, their armpits glowing with fine sweat
has vagabonding   settled the destiny of darkness?
       SON   a road that won't let you go is
       exact enough   fabulous enough   life's castle in the air
       floating in a minute that no one notices

十、银链子
（插曲）

深深拔　银制的密语

深深　环环相扣的铮亮日子　拔
自肉中那枚摸不到底的洞

夏天的湖岸上阳光锻造一只锚
我们摇曳　水的耳语也在
床上　水痕一波波舔向
细腰捧起的妖媚的肉窝儿
动　银子一股股绞紧
脚尖钩住脚尖的金属绳
拔呀　无视你的娇嫩

自又一年散开时拔璀璨诀别的一吻

美如一首弦乐的湖岸休止不了
我们踱步　密语的质地切断不了
夏天的焦点如此夺目
被两只妖冶的翅膀死死护着
显示荷花的要害
自己都惊恐　一种
仍然盯着水面的韧性

仍在毕生提炼着纠缠之美　铆定
耻骨与耻骨环环相扣的零

拔　　出　　血分子里碇泊的一朵荷花

180

10 Silver chain

(Interlude)

pluck deep deep   secret words made of silver

deep deep   interlocking days polished till they shine   pluck
from the bottomless pit in the flesh

on summer's lakeside the sun forges an anchor
we bob and rock   the water's whispers are also
on the bed   ripples lap one by one towards
the ravishing flesh-nest a slender waist lifts
moves   each tightly twisted silver strand
a metal rope where tiptoe catches on tiptoe
oh pluck   ignore your tender fragility

pluck an incandescent goodbye kiss from when another year dispersed

lakeside lovely as string music can't stop
our sauntering   the texture of secret words can't interrupt
summer's focus dazzling this way
tightly guarded by two seductive wings
displaying the lotus blossom's vital spot
itself all panic-stricken   a kind of
doggedness still staring at the water's surface

refining as before beauty entangled   riveted
pubis to pubis an interlocked zero

pluck   out   the lotus blossom moored in molecules of blood

十一、路

蝉声以诵经众僧的俯仰之势吟哦
茫茫的美学　一条街泛滥着清晨
三颗星种植在我墨玉的额头上
哦蝉声　吟哦摧毁时间的美学
走在时间里的那人脱掉多余的部分
觉得沁凉的重量从绿叶间移到
压住的舌尖上　一块玉叫嚷无声
昆虫的小小颅骨支起天空的拱顶
哦茫茫就是一个人和宇宙并肩上路
哦东方就是任酷热的蓝贯穿彼此
锁骨就锁住了万古愁　地上地下
我扇着一对丝织的翅膀　仙人之美
就是孤绝到极点　环湖中路上
我模仿父亲每天把脚步放慢一点
红砖楼群模仿海上嶙峋的巨石
夹击　汹涌的　探亲的一只蝉
无处来也无处去　除了
有个和舌头雕刻在一起的硬度
泥土中探出的舌头　捣毁呼号
径直　歌唱突入死亡内部的现实

11 Road

cicadas declaim in the bent posture of scripture-chanting monks
aesthetics of vast emptiness   a street overflowing with the dawn
three stars planted on my black jade brow
oh cicada song   recite the aesthetic that destroys time
someone who travels in time strips surplus parts away
feeling a cooling weight shift from among the green leaves to
the tamped-down tongue   a lump of jade silently bellows
tiny insect skulls prop up the vault of the sky
oh the vast emptiness is a man setting out shoulder to shoulder with the universe
oh the East is letting sweltering blues interpenetrate each other
collarbones locking up every ancient sorrow   above and below ground
I flap silken wings   the beauty of immortality
is solitary in the extreme   on Lakeside Road
I copy father's daily-slower steps
crowded red-brick buildings imitate craggy boulders in the seas
a pincer movement   a raging   a cicada visiting home
comes from nowhere and goes nowhere   unless
there's the hardness that's carved along with a tongue
a tongue stretching out from the earth   a demolished distress call
directly   singing a reality that enters deep inside death

十二、叙事诗

没有一个街角　　路牌　　车站
不在检举我们　　像语言

没有一株垂柳不在收紧碧绿的网
圈住疯狂转向的鱼群

让称之为故乡的　　游动冤魂的情节
被体内钙化的雪驱逐到烈日下

柏油青烟袅袅　　云中之鬼
热衷一张从反面冲洗世界的负片

烘烤一个考古学中
蒸发不完的　　雕栏画栋的此刻

想召唤就召唤出满街浓浓的肉色
想终结就终结　　像母亲

躲进一把黄白色的骨灰
早已写下的芳香　　摆在我案头

叙述体温那件事　　血压那件事
漆黑峰顶上一颗流星为我们摔碎那件事

摔碎无力说出任何东西的眼睛
一块老玉修炼亿万年

精选出诗这唯一一件事
无言的结构剥开无数哭喊的方言

绕过星空　　朝父亲漫步
还原为寓意本身

12 Narrative Poem

there's not a street corner   street name   bus stop
that doesn't inform on us   like languages

there's not a weeping willow not drawing the green net tight
to encircle shoals of fish that dart crazily to and fro

let it be called the hometown's   storyline of wandering ghosts done wrong
snow calcified in the body banished to below a burning sun

black asphalt smoke curling up   the ghosts in the clouds
crave negatives that will develop the world from its obverse

roast in archaeology a still-unevaporated
instant   of carved columns and painted beams

if you want to summon then summon the flesh tints glutting the street
if you want to end it then end it   like a mother

hide in a handful of yellow-white ashes
a perfume long ago written down   set on my desk

the thing about narrating body temperature   the thing about blood pressure
the thing about a fallen star that shattered above a jet-black summit for us

shattered and fallen with eyes that have no strength to speak
a lump of jade millions of years in monastic asceticism

carefully choose this one and only thing about poetry
wordless structures strip bare countless dialects of weeping and wailing

bypass the starry firmament   slow steps towards father
return to their origin as the moral of the story itself

水薄荷叙事诗（五）

——哀歌，和李商隐

WATERMINT NARRATIVE 5

Elegies, after Li Shangyin[32]

---

32. Li Shangyin (*c.* 813-858) is one of the great Late Tang Dynasty poets. Everything in italics is a quotation from his work. Yang Lian has provided this finding list:

有感（非关宋玉有微辞）
楚吟
无题四首·其一（来是空言去**绝踪**）
落花
代应二首·其一（**沟水分流西复东**）
房中曲
水天**闲话**旧事
楚**宫**（湘波如泪色**滢滢**）／嫦娥

"一自高唐赋成后
楚天云雨尽堪疑"

而楚天恰是多云多雨的
而昨夜星辰昨夜风　唯一隔着
两个字之间的清霜

而谁在踱步？一只船泊进
水上水下两个世界

双重的茫茫　　他的香
叹冷我们的流水

一湾暗绿吞吞　　吐吐
舔过油漆成黑色的铁船壳
一种老橡木的明黄色　攥紧
老式方形的舷窗　窗纱后
他的假寐　切入小公园死寂的草色

他停下的音节劈开句子的千江月
水的长街上　鸟翅逐一抹去
风暴的理由　鸟嘴啄空
一粒野浆果的艳红被灌木铁丝网
圈禁的理由

茫茫　波浪无岸的呵护
他的凛冽中
还有什么没写尽？

而我们早就像一个疑问一样
存在　当你记得的河谷秋意更深
一幅楚天逸出挽入水声的长发
云和雨　隔着摆成一千年的思想

读吧　所有诗剥开都是爱情诗

＊　＊　＊

188

When once the High Pond Rhapsody was done
The cloud and rain in Southland skies were all the wonder they could bear

yet in Southland skies many clouds much rain
yet *last night's stars and last night's wind*   the only things dividing
the clear frost between two words

and who is pacing to and fro? a boat anchors in
the two worlds above and below the water

twofold vastness and vastness   his incense
sighs our flowing water chilly

an all dark-green river-bend gobbles   spews
laps by the black-painted hull
that kind of clear old oak yellow   clutches tight
the antique square portholes   behind the window gauze
his siesta   mows the deathly still grass-green of the little park

syllables he stopped split open the line's *moon on a thousand rivers*
on the long street of the water   birds' wings erase the excuses of
gales one by one   beaks peck
the scarlet of a wild berry poured into a barbed-wire bush
an excuse for being caged

vast vast   the blessing of shoreless waves
in his bitter piercing cold
what else was left unwritten?

and we have long been like a doubt, a question
existing   as the valley you remembered grows more deeply autumnal
long hair escaping Southland skies and fleeing to the water's sound
clouds and rain   divided by thoughts that set out a thousand years

read then   all poems peeled open are love poems

*   *   *

"山上离宫宫上楼
楼前宫畔暮江流"

而最美的爱情诗必是一首赠别诗

非诀别不可　　一封信
踩着千年间所有最后一瞥
非无视无题怎样提炼暮色的粘稠不可
我攀登过的那座荒台
非得拆毁成纯粹远去的你

性欲的纯粹颜色
皮肤在万丈悬崖上萦漾浅黑
抱不到时湛蓝发亮
一次摔碎凿刻一道错金的水面

都醒在梦中　　他写比云更远的梦中梦
我们被一堆乱石早早望见
夜夜　　王　　饮着不可能的毒酒解渴

唯美　　就是爱上不可能本身
叠字清音波荡　　逼人掉头而去

＊　＊　＊

"书被催成墨未浓"

就这样我们摇曳在千年墨色中
推移　　河谷写成的天鹅的倒影
洁白羽毛覆盖着暴力　　水声的
哀筝衔接满巫峡草茎的急管
更换一只老船里紧贴板壁的耳朵
抽血一样抽走日子　　哪个
是不能翻译成音乐的？偷听相思
与灰烬　　何必问贯穿谁的节奏？

190

A palace on the mountain, a tower upon the palace
Before the tower the palace moat, the twilight river flowing

and the most beautiful love poem must be a poem of farewell

we can't help but say farewell   an epistle
treads on every final glance in thousands of years
must be the unseen *Untitled* in how it refines dusk's density
the deserted terrace I once climbed to
must be demolished to be the you who are purely gone away

the pure colour of desire
skin tangled in rippling tan on towering cliffs
when it can't be embraced the azure shine
fallen once and shattered it carves water gold-inlaid

all wake in dreams   he writes a dream in a dream farther than clouds
we were early on spied by a pile of rubble
night by night   a king   drinks the poisoned wine of impossibility to slake
his thirst

aestheticism   is falling in love with impossibility itself
reduplicated unvoiced sounds heave and surge   forcing us to turn and go

*   *   *

In books finished by force, the ink has not darkened

just so do we teeter in a thousand years of ink
evolve   a swan's river-valley-written reflection
feathers spotlessly white conceal violence   the sound of the water's
mourning harp is yoked to the urgent piping of Shaman Gorge's grass blades
changing the ear glued to an old boat's wooden wall
draw away the days like drawing blood   which day
cannot be translated into music?   eavesdrop on love-longing
and ashes   what need to ask whose rhythm they pierce?

191

我们轻轻磕碰石岸　足音淋漓
令游客回头　这墨色
研了千年仍不够浓
绷直一根绿绿油腻的柳丝

就这样我们用五首哀歌互相道别
和自己道别　五个辞行的长句
给一条河一个慢慢倾吐出的结构
一盏会作曲的烛火埋在水下
用五种腥味分解一条鱼
五条乐谱线平行于早晨的鸟鸣
每条攥着一种玲珑的听觉
每阵雁叫装订一本回眸的书
河水翻找潜藏肉里的一枚枚冬至
烧制一件落不上红叶的青瓷
就是挥别了　身边这道涟漪
总是蓬山万重外最后一场冷雨

就这样归纳为狂想　掏空辞
辞才被说出　不改呼吸的密码
诗才等同一种窒息　我们不信任的
语言归纳我们抓不住的生命
虚无绝美　你径直拣起这本书
他留下的船标点逝水
我打磨一面面无关月光的圆圆镜子
那不怕摔碎的　满抱没有瞬间的
珊瑚　水母　彩色盲目的小鱼
写下一首诗　世界已可以消失

*　*　*

we knock lightly against the stony shore   the dripping of footsteps
makes travellers turn their heads   this ink
ground a thousand years and still not darkened enough
straightens a twig of greasy green willow-floss

just so we bid farewell to each other with five elegies
and bid ourselves farewell   five long lines of leave-taking
give the river a structure that has been pouring slowly out
a music-making candle flame is buried underwater
dismantles fish with five fishy reeks
five lines of musical score parallel morning's birdsong
each one clutches an exquisitely agile kind of hearing
every goose's honk binds a book of backward glances
river water rummaging for every tiny winter solstice hidden in flesh
fires a celadon piece no red leaves can fall on
that's what waving goodbye is   the ripples alongside
always the final cold rain past Paradise Hill's endless ridges

just so is conclusion a vain dream   all words hollowed out
a word only spoken   doesn't change breath's secret password
only then is poetry equal to the same suffocation   language
we don't trust concludes the life we cannot grasp
nothingness absolutely beautiful   you pick this book right up
the boat he left behind punctuates never-returning water
I polish round round mirrors with no relation to moonlight
unafraid to fall and shatter   hugging momentless
coral   jellyfish   little colour-blind fish
writing down a poem   and the world can disappear

*   *   *

"小园花乱飞"
"所得是沾衣"

活埋在玉米田里的阶级敌人感到
钢筋和打桩机　　滋长阴谋的胡子
一只水泥小瓮盛满尿　　淅沥的雨声不变
而发酸的外语品牌的春天浇湿总转到脚下的星球
对于现实　　我们知道些什么？

情人最初的白发短短　　细细　　镜中如此娇嫩
另一个女孩沿着银色的索道滑行
女儿的更苍老的女儿　　被捻着
像缕鼻息　　旅馆浴室中从身后满捧乳房的手
哈气般散去　　窗外夜空的一朵莲花散去
对于爱情　　我们知道些什么？

海岸上僵直盯视水平线的动物
垂下化石的眉毛　　云恰似又一个朝代咳嗽
蜇进腔肠　　虽然迟暮传染病在皮肤上挤满疣斑
可对于历史　　我们知道些什么？

一个人里面是一群人　　远远走着
每条路绘出美人儿的曲线
一群人　　忙忙引用一个子宫湿润肥沃的出处
因为赎不回出处　　美人儿娇喘吁吁
用乱伦的欢叫拉长地平线　　像徽宗放飞的鹤
对于故乡　　我们知道些什么？

除了一个字　　像座高阁目送着客人
像个漩涡　　不停自终点内剥出终点
问　　还有多少黑暗录制在一次激情里
急急铲除天边的积雪　　拂净白纸上手之落花
对于诗　　我们知道些什么？

＊　　＊　　＊

Flowers flew wild in the little garden
What you got was wet clothes

the class enemy buried alive in the cornfield can feel
reinforcing bars and pile-drivers   growing a beard of conspiracies
a concrete jar filled with piss   the patter of rain unchanged
and spring with its sour foreign brand is watering stars that forever turn underfoot
REALITY   what do we know of it?

short short a lover's first white hair   fine fine   so delicate in the mirror
another girl slides across the silver rope bridge
a daughter's more aging daughter   twisted
like a breath   in the hotel bathroom hands from behind full of breasts
dissolve like sighs   outside the window the lotuses of the night sky dissolve
LOVE   what do we know of it?

animals on the seashore stare stiffly at the horizon
lower fossil eyebrows   clouds like another dynasty's cough
re-enter the body cavity   though dusk's infection has covered the skin with warts
but HISTORY   what do we know of it?

there is a crowd inside a person   going far far away
every road paints the curves of a beautiful woman
a crowd   busy citing the womb's moist fertile source
because a source can't be ransomed   beauty gasps delicately for breath
stretches the skyline with incestuous pleasure-cries   like the cranes Huizong[35] freed
HOME   what do we know of it?

except for one word   like a high tower watching guests leave
like a whirlpool   endlessly peeling destination from destination
ask   how much dark still recording in a one-time driven passion
hurries to shovel snow from the sky's edge
sweeps a hand's fallen flowers from the white paper?
POETRY   what do we know of it?

*   *   *

33. Emperor of the Song dynasty (*r.* 1100-1126).

"十二玉楼空更空"

我一次次从空中张望这片水
机翼抚过北伦敦　家何在？
一长串绘制云影的内脏形反光何在？
一座花园是一块绿色斑斓的锈
缓缓退去的树林退还给水蛇的沼泽
幽暗树梢背后一片诡谲的红光何在？
（贝尔　冰川的黑舌磨擦你的章句
晓渡　大风夜的灌木越无灯越明媚
帕斯卡尔　译诗必经的河谷
必然是无底的）玉楼升高
十二层　水薄荷中亡灵吟唱
孤单夜游的天鹅拖曳她的三角浪
一个邀我认出的涵义何在？揩干
署名的角度　从空中踩碎黄白色固体
机翼揭开一望无边的盐碛

*　　*　　*

"归来已不见
锦瑟长于人"

一首赠别诗从８５９年写到２００８年
李商隐　他的梧桐数尽盘旋的凤凰
他的女道友——羽化为绝望的韵脚
他弥留时眼中的蓝　收拢一生
泼溅到笔下的血迹

　　我们的血迹　不做梦的人梦见了
　　最美的山顶上嘴对嘴呼喊的雾
　　引渡河谷一夜刷白车窗玻璃的雾
　　你从十页纸的小论文到一个吻
　　得进化多少年？指尖嘘着寒意的一触
　　否决永远就到了不解冻的永远
　　写多苯　那就别写　这个冬天

again and again I have seen this stretch of water from the air
the plane's wings stroking over North London   home is where?
a long string of viscera-shaped reflections painting cloud-shadow is where?
a garden is a piece of variegated green rust
gently withdrawing woods return to water-snake swamps
a weird red glow behind dark twigs is where?
Bill Herbert   the glacier's dark tongue scours your chapter and verse
Tang Xiaodu   bushes in windy night the more lampless the brighter they get
Pascale Petit   the inevitable river valley of translating poems
is necessarily bottomless   jade pavilions rise higher
twelve stories   lost souls chant in the watermint
a solitary night-swimming swan trails its triangular wake
the meaning I'm asked to know is where?   wipe clean
the angles of the signature   trample and break the yellow-white solids
the plane's wings reveal salt deserts as far as the eye can see

*   *   *

Returned but still unseen
The brocade zither lasts longer than a man

a farewell poem written to the year 2008 from the year 859
Li Shangyin   his sycamores have counted all the circling phoenixes
his Taoist lady friends transmogrified one by one to rhymes of despair
blue in his deathbed eyes   gathered a whole life's
bloodstains spattering under his writing-brush

    our bloodstains   those dreamless ones have seen in dreams
    mist roaring mouth-to-mouth on the loveliest mountaintops
    transform river valley mist on car windows painted silver overnight
    for you to arrive at a kiss from a little ten-page thesis
    needs how many years of evolution? fingertip contact breathes a chill
    on overruled forever then arrives at unthawing forever
    writing is so stupid   so don't write then   this winter

完成的冷　让一首诗潺潺沉在水下
都是雾　环抱中震荡的裸体也是
谁梦见谁就回来

忧伤的诗何时才吐尽忧伤？如他
四十八岁的画舫载不动的　大醉的
他燃在琴台上的那炷香复述不出
她们那缕烟　他的墓草青青
如水仙　吹奏一根粉红色的鲜肉笛子
过多的人生　过多的无力

　　我们的无力　把回来的情节变成
　　一次星际旅行　你乳头上的香
　　隔开一分钟已是株轮回的植物
　　一个渐渐浑圆的腰身带着结局的惊恐
　　眺望一双温存的手　一再
　　丢失进修辞　这本书径直拣起我们
　　听清深夜嘎嘎的开片声
　　每天建造的裂缝里　哪个青春
　　不是晦暗的　虚掷的？年年朗诵
　　时间的空白　用我们
　　带在身上的终点淹没他的终点
　　枕着的水波汩汩流淌　诗恒碧
　　诗人心甘情愿骑乘着陨石

　　　　　　　　＊　＊　＊

　　　　"暮雨自归山悄悄"

一首诗是我们拿生命抵押的全部
一首诗　阴户边缘微微烧焦着
繁殖劫数　迫使一次赠别愈加色情
哪座荒台不是巫峡旁我登临的那座？
雨后的燕子穿缝断简　残云　王梦
荒台即祭台？你我本来就是传说

198

cold fulfilled   makes a poem sink babbling under water
it's all mists   a shuddering nakedness in an embrace is too
whoever dreams will return

when will a poem of grief vomit up all the grief?   like what
his painted pleasure boat of forty-eight years couldn't carry dead drunk
the stick of incense he burned on the zither stand couldn't repeat
the female wisp of their smoke   his grave green with grass
like narcissus   blowing a pink flute of flesh
far too many human lives   far too much powerlessness

     our powerlessness   turns the story of coming back into
     a journey between stars   the incense on your nipples
     after a minute's separation is a plant reincarnated
     a waist growing rounder bears the terror of endings
     gazing at two gentle hands   again and again
     lost in the rhetoric   this book picks us up directly
     to hear clearly the crackle of the crazing
     in daily manufactured cracks   what youth
     isn't dark?   wasted?   reciting year after year
     time's blankness   using the end-point
     we carry on our body to drown his end-point
     pillowing waves gurgling flow   poems forever aquamarine
     a poet is always willing to ride the meteor

*   *   *

Coming back alone in the evening rain, the mountains were silent

a poem is all of the life we mortgaged
a poem   burning faintly at the vagina's edge
breeds a doom   forces a one-time farewell to be even more erotic
what deserted terrace isn't the one I climbed by Shaman Gorge?
rainy swallows pierce and stitch broken bamboo   lingering clouds   a king's
                                         dream
was the deserted terrace an altar?   you and I are tales from the start

被日夜流淌弄真了　悬崖下错金的河
目睹交出自己的形式

一首诗教我们实习一种死亡
哪首不是这首？你眼睛的年关
注视更深时　山中的静注射得更深
我不舍的是爱还是内分泌的茫茫？
桌子撒向远方的血肉都有湿淋淋
女性的语法　祭祀的大海固执于
一株拒绝移过新年的野茶树　长成
谎言伤害不了的形式

＊　　＊　　＊

"女萝山鬼语相邀"

"碧海青天夜夜心"

李商隐可以是一只船的名字
刚刚下水的　还不知过去未来的
船坞里一方小小的波浪　摇荡
共时之蓝　金属的婴儿皮肤上
幻觉之蓝　吊车的鹤向下观望
星期日的大洋停顿着

一个离乱世纪的休止符
自离乱的阳光渗出　那船体雪白
那沉睡巨大　那等待把一只海鸥
派遣为隐喻　代替风中解体的人
船舷上一盏灯无缘无故亮着
照耀一堆无缘无故衍生的钢铁

水薄荷都有劈开风声的船头
岁月什么也不说　只听头上
某位鬼魂作曲家叫着　笑着　玩
一个每天的零被海平线整理成型

made real by the flow of nights and days   the river gold-inlaid below the cliffs
is eye-witness to the shape of a surrendering self

a poem teaches us to practise a kind of death
what poem isn't this one?   when the year-end of your eyes
gazes deeper   the mountain silence is injected deeper
is it love I grudge or the vastness of hormones?
all the flesh and blood a desk spills into the distance has a drenched
feminine grammar   the ocean of sacrifice clings to
a wild tea bush refusing to move into the new year   grows up
into a shape lies cannot hurt

*   *   *

If a woman dream of mountain spirits, her words will invite them

Green sea, blue sky, night after night, a heart

Li Shangyin could be the name of a boat
new-launched   not yet knowing past or future
tiny square of waves in the harbour   rocking
simultaneous blue   on the skin of the metal infant
hallucinatory blue   cranes bend their heads to look down
on Sunday's   great ocean standstill

the silent beat in a century of disaster and division
leaks out from the sunshine of disaster and division   the boat's hull snow-white
gigantic that sleep   the waiting sends out
seagulls as metaphors   to replace people disintegrating in the wind
on the boat's flank for no reason a lamp is burning
lighting a pile of steel generated for no reason

all watermint has a prow that cleaves the wind's noise
months and years don't say a thing   only listen to
some ghost composer howling at the prow   laughing   playing with
an every-day zero tidied by the horizon into its shape

一架小风琴　他的　却招我
饮一杯　两个时代的浊酒

共用一场醉　两首赠别诗
分享一个加速储存黑暗自我的语言
不分彼此　一页碧蓝的乐谱
挪动某只被演奏的书写的手
分不出彼此　水上水下双重茫茫
累断彩凤双飞翼　哪儿有彼此？

除了一颗心　鬼魂似的邀请
离乱的美学　李商隐钻出又一个浪
李河谷预约了油漆拍碎的归来的
死　我们的重逢也造好了
和自己告别是每一刹那的事
译成风的无辞歌是同一刹那的事

夜的无题诗　夜夜美艳
那会流淌的银子　涂掉流过的痕迹
非模拟皮肤上一片爱恋的光泽不可
推开情人的触摸　一个躯体
渗漏进另一躯体　航向
不可能的　刺耳的　肉欲的　深

鬼魂作曲家早已设定的结构
非模拟水不可　一丛水薄荷
清清的苦　苦苦的香
非完成整个存在不可　船和人
诞生就是诗的隐喻　诗祭奠
仍是一次手牵女萝终古交尾的隐喻

我们都在　一篇
王梦过就再也难忘的长赋中
被加工成一朵云之聚散
一群星之起落　楚天上纵横
做爱的轨道迷醉于精液芬芳之蓝的
音　乐　会

a little harmonium   his   but it beckons me
to quaff a goblet   the cloudy wine of two eras

sharing the same drunkenness two farewell poems
share an idiolect stored faster and faster in darkness
no mine and no yours   a page of indigo sheet music
moving some writing hand that is performed
can't tell mine or yours   twofold vastness above and below the water
continually breaks the motley phoenix's beating wings   where are yours and mine?

except for a heart   a ghostly invitation
aesthetics of disaster and division   Li Shangyin unscrews another wave
the Lee Valley has booked a paint-shattered returning
death   our reunion has also created it
saying goodbye to yourself is a matter for every instant
a poem's wordless song translated into wind is a matter for the same instant

night's untitled poems   gorgeous night after night
the silver that can flow   blots out the scars of flowing
it has to imitate the sheen of love on the skin
pushing away a lover's touch   a body
leaks into another body   its course towards
impossible   earsplitting   carnal   depth

the structure a ghost composer long ago set up
must simulate water   a clump of watermint
clear fresh bitterness   bitter bitter incense
must complete the whole of existence   boat and man
birth is poetry's metaphor   poetry offers a libation
is still a metaphor for guiding lichen and moss to mate forever

we are all in   a long rhapsody
once dreamed by a King and now unforgettable
worked into the gathering and dispersing of cloud
the rising and setting of stars   the length and breadth of the Southland skies
the track of lovemaking drunk on a semen-perfumed blue
C O N C E R T

第三部

哲人之墟：共时·无梦

（小快板）

PART 3

RUIN OF SAGES.SYNCHRONIC.DREAMLESS

(*Allegretto*)

置换之墟

暴风雨掷过头顶　航班又一次取消
窗外竖起的海面　数着
玻璃上坠毁的碎石声
时刻表无尽拉长一个此刻
尖尖翘起的停飞的机翼
抖动时速八十英里的候机室
如忧郁症抖动一个女孩儿

一只等候的小沙发陷下
不多不少现实的深度
读完一本小说需要不多不少
晚点的生活的语速　一排巨浪
撞碎　让你从一根试管中窥望
一场万云澎湃的绝望的化学反应
水泥跑道孤零零滑翔

天空黑暗审视的眼神下
女孩儿舔着药味的唇
你舔报废的瓢泼的
方向　砸着岸
一个坍塌在躯体中的重量
析出耳畔失重的声音
"改期还是退票，先生？"

Ruin of replacement

the storm tosses overhead   another flight cancelled
the perpendicular sea outside the windows   counts
the crash of gravel on the windows
the timetable endlessly stretches this moment out
grounded wings turn sharply up
shake the airport lounge at eighty miles per hour
like depression shaking a young girl

a waiting armchair bogged down in
the depth of neither too much or too little reality
finishing a novel needs neither too much or too little
the tempo of a life running late   wave after huge wave
shattering   make you spy from inside a test-tube
the chemical reaction of despair in a million surging clouds
the concrete runway gliding in lonely isolation

under the sky's dark scrutinising eye
a girl licks lips that taste of medicine
you lick a junked torrential
direction   hammering the shore
a caved-in weight in the body
analyses the weightless sound in the ears
'Will you change your flight or return your ticket, sir?'

银之墟（一）

一只瓶比爱的转折快　带走
细心镂刻的雾霭　密林　山岫
沿着小径　溪水向下　你向上
都是视线的游戏　擦亮流淌

甚至不留下流淌的痕迹
比白昼快　那修饰你腰肢的力
拉紧黑暗天空中那些星子
隐居的云海闪闪烁烁满是词

挂在你小屋前　五六只雨燕
缓缓生锈　把世界再遗弃一遍
每天醒来的作品　肌肤如银
空茫海水下空置的岩石都如银

听　远古的首饰匠叮叮锤打
你回避　比被捧出更像一朵花
金属沉入废除一生的假寐
废正是意义　坠着金色的耳垂

瓶抖开光的璀璨瀑布
一道小径排练冲刷声的歌剧
溪水白亮亮向下　昔日在臆想中
你摘掉自我向上　一种抒情

云一样高　漫过对面的山脊时
历史一无所求如逆向的性欲
轻拂这瓶　比镂刻的西风薄
你忘了身上滑落过多少颜色

Ruin of silver 1

a vase is faster than love's alterations   takes
painstakingly engraved mists   deep woods   peaks
along the little path   the stream runs down   up you go
it's all a visual game   burnishing the gleam of the flow

till not even a trace of the flow is left
faster than daylight's alteration   the strength your back adorning
pulls those particles in the dark sky tight
in the hermit's cloud-ocean it's all words shimmering

hanging before your small room   five or six swifts
progressively tarnishing   abandon the world again
an opus that wakes each day   skin like silver
vacant rocks like silver beneath the void seawater

hear   the tap of the ancient silversmith hammering
you withdraw   more flower-like than flattering
metal sunk in a siesta that repeals lifespans
repeal is significant   as it weighs down golden earlobes

a glorious waterfall of light shaken by a vase
a little path rehearsing the opera of erosion
a stream running down brilliantly white   the olden days in a notion
you detach self as you go up   a kind of lyric verse

high as the clouds   spilling over the opposite mountain
like desire in reverse history seeks nothing
caress this vase   flimsier than the engraved west wind
you have forgotten how many colours once slid over your skin

银之墟（二）

山花野果要什么名字？她说
她抬起眼睛　三十年前的清波
漾着香　取代花蕊那缕香
山之蕊　一瓣瓣剥开诗行

眺望中仍未完全变黑的下午
夜还在收紧悬崖　临风处
一潭水泛起暗色满浸寒意
从脚下　把你驱逐进一点余晖

认识的反面银光闪闪
擎着针　扎穿鸟鸣奔逃的蓝
深处亮起的灯火剜去山字
骨髓里阵阵疼剜去冷字

而银不是字　是挽紧发髻的空
山气弥漫中她的眼睛
山路般陡峭　一双麻鞋
留一枚让你无尽抽丝的茧子

抽　一种不得不爱上的阴柔
摩擦粉红色　哦一个隘口
要什么名字？裸露隐匿都是美
偃月冠下一世界阅读不尽的美

一声反问来自满枝如雪的花朵
折断三十年　那儿没人说
断的香　爱你就性你　百万次
死过的名字都这样成为真的

Ruin of silver 2

what names do mountain flowers and wild fruit need? she says
she lifts her eyes   from thirty years back limpid sprays
brim with fragrance   supplanting the fragrance of the pistil
the mountain's stamens   peel open lines of verse petal by petal

looking at afternoon not yet completely blackened
night still tightening the cliff   facing the wind
dark that floats up from the pond gives the cold a soaking
from underfoot   drives you into the last of the gloaming

silver shines on the other side of understanding
holding a needle   to pierce birdsong's bolted indigo
lamps lighting the deep gouge out the word *mountain*
spasms of pain gouge the word *cold* from bone marrow

but silver is not a word   it's the emptiness of tight chignons
her eyes in the all-pervading mist on the mountains
sheer as mountain tracks   a pair of straw sandals
leave your endlessly unwinding silk cocoons

unwind   a feminine gentleness you can't not adore
rub pinkness   oh a mountain pass
what name does it need?   naked and hidden are both lovely
crowned with a Taoist cap you'll never read all the world's beauty

one question back from flowers on every snow-white bough
break off thirty years   nobody there said
fragrance of excision   loving you genders you   a million times
so names that once were dead become real now

银之墟（三）

慵懒的枪倚在唇边
睨视　　一株汗腺浸湿的水仙
细细的狐狸味儿被追捕到底
是不屑逃走的味儿　　轻抚醉意

枪口似的几乎睡着了
袅袅的玩具轻烟　　玩具般扫射
一缕亲手包裹成行李的体香
一把杀生的雪　　杀　　他的远方

墨就是雪　　一对锦绣书童
合穿一件夜行衣　　诗是征程
两片月色护着他的万里外
和你的阳台　　一朵云的迷彩

给一扇纸窗安上诀别夜
无所谓错的方向　　让嗅觉
倚着你体内人生唯一的方向
"心疼"那个词　　一声枪响

你终是没有忘　　而他炫目
如背对阴阳的挺立的干尸
唇间天涯镇快递一根仙草
到酒乡　　血淋淋吻　　血淋淋笑

血丝儿沁的汗意射穿那人
秋　　啊　　秋凉最适养心
枪口滑落　　雪　　潜望着归来
读懂世界那滴墨　　躺进洁白

Ruin of silver 3

leaning by the lips a languid gun
looks askance at   sweat-gland-drenched narcissus
a delicate foxy aroma hunted to the end
it's a smell not worth escaping   lightly stroking drunkenness

the muzzle seems slumbering almost
curling toy smoke   a toy-like barrage
a whiff of body odour a personally-packed baggage
a handful of murderous snow   kills   his far distance

ink is snow   a pair of embroidered pageboys
sharing a ninja outfit   poetry is a voyage
two moonlights guard his *ten thousand miles away*[34]
with your balcony   a cloud's camouflage

fit on window paper a night of farewell
no odds if the direction's wrong   let sense of smell
lean on life's only direction within you
the words *heartbreaking love*   a gunshot

you have not been forgotten after all   but his glamour
is like a mummy standing with its back to Yin and Yang
a stalk of fairy grass on the lips World's End Town will deliver
to Boozeborough   blood-drenched smile   blood-drenched kiss

sweat from oozing veins pierce that man through
autumn   oh   best for heart's ease is autumn cool
the gun muzzle slips   snow   spies on homecoming
reads the ink-drop of the world   in spotless white reclining

------

34. Gao Shi (704-765), *Seeing Censor Li off to the Far West*: 'rank and fame ten thousand miles away, heart's cares in one glass'.

哲人之墟

他们可能只不过在谈论山羊
缓缓啜一口茶　浓了暮色
连成一片的松针上漂着月亮

松香味儿的大树稳稳撑着
四合的山影　泼掉一日鸟声
一张青石凳反锁游客

谛听中　他们被口音剔净
一只瓷茶杯沉淀如玉的远方
轻轻放下时仍温润而透明

Ruin of Sages

maybe they were just talking about sheep
leisurely sipping tea   in the gathering gloaming
and into moonlight on pine needles floating

great pine-scented trees strengthening
hill shadows all around   spill all day with birds singing
a limestone bench locks visitors in

in true listening   they are filleted by words
a china teacup was distant sand now settled into jade
gently put down   still translucent and warm

锡拉库札诗群：生之墟

一

等在终点上的雨也锤痛起点
大港深邃如耳廓　　防波堤迎向
青铜镶嵌的雨声　　旅馆窗台下
溅开的绣花披肩围着秀丽的肩膀
一种拨动石头流淌的雕刻艺术
还给大海时　　等在浪花中的乳房
向你突起　　雨织入款款的衣褶
一件灰白沉思的袍子从窗口
覆盖到床上　　让睡眠不停出海
听到你　　一点点漏出古老的梦呓

二

雨线的铁链从天而降　　扣紧
语言　　你加速储存的漆黑自我
四月的石壁上又一柄凿子
加深囚徒们绝望抓出的指痕
床还在这儿　　你肉做的石坑
囚禁着哭喊　　说出就在追逐潮水
写　　海藻中沉船就深深起伏
又一朵锁在追悼上的浪碎了
又一座胜利纪念碑踩着磷光返航
任何语言里四月都是断壁残垣

三

但你得自己走一次　　淋湿一次
感受一个夭折的胎儿像海豚潜泳
绕过珊瑚一点点融入海水的墨绿色
一百三十六天暴露袖珍的女儿
一颗谢绝成型的小心脏解散成
波纹的弧度　　一绺黑发甜甜改编
不透明的历史　　大海碧蓝的砖缝间
有只蜥蜴金绿色的眼珠返回
用最小瞪着最大　　眺望的海面
把世界像条多余的尾巴一口咬掉

216

Syracusan verses: Ruin of a life

1

rain waiting at the terminus also hammers the start
a great harbour deep as an ear   breakwaters greet
the bronze-inlaid sound of rain   under the hotel window
a spattered tapestry shawl wraps pretty shoulders
the art of carving that churns the stones' flow
returned to the sea   the breast waiting in the breakers
springs up towards you   rain woven into slow folds
a gown of grey thought spread from window
to bed   makes sleep endlessly set sail
hears you   leak out bit by bit from ancient sleep-talk

2

iron shackles of rain fall from the sky   fetter
language   you speed to store your jet black self
one more chisel on April's stone wall
deepening prisoners' finger-marks dug in anguish
bed still here   the stone pit made of your flesh
howls in prison   to speak is to chase the tidewater
to write   shipwrecks deep in seaweed rise and fall
one more wave locked in mourning will now shatter
one more victory monument trampling phosphorus-light will sail for harbour
April in any tongue is ruined rampart and broken wall

3

but you must go once yourself   be soaking wet once
feel an aborted foetus like the dolphin's plunge
bypass coral to melt a little into the dark green of seawater
one hundred and thirty-six days reveal a pocket-sized daughter
a little heart that refused to take form dissolves into
an arc of ripples   one lock of black hair sweetly adapted to
an opaque history   between joins on the ocean's indigo brick
are a lizard's green and gold eyes turning back
staring at the biggest with the smallest   the sea observing from far away
bites the world off in one mouthful like an unnecessary tail

217

四

在雅典　诗人帕特里求斯呻吟"够了"
公元前四二三年的雨对头颅够了
亶耗的颈椎断了　大理石的巢
弃置松针间　惨白溃烂着思想够了
祭坛上公牛屠宰前阵阵哀鸣
刺激春草　死者发苦的清香
为了谁又挂满旅游手册的枝头？
咽喉埋进电喇叭能抚慰什么？
希腊语的眼窝里海是一把干透的
尘土　太痛苦了　别折磨亡灵了

五

但你的亡灵在身上不安波动
锁着划桨的蓝像只开屏的孔雀
比绝壁高一点　比历史高一点
亮晶晶填充坠毁一滴雨的重量
一个胎儿和七千拍卖的奴隶列队
比沙石小径低一点　更低
哭声从地下握住趿着凉鞋的脚
你雕成一个拼命仰望的样子服刑
蓝远得像家　海底无限沉溺
一滴雨落了千年还没触到你的脸上

六

一场锡拉库札的雨混淆了时间
在书中下　组成文笔冷冷下
你眼中总有座在移开的雕花窗台
带着墙头濡湿红艳的蔷薇
那裸露双乳的女人迎面走过
残破的字虚掩一团怯生生的肉
时间打着皮肤而你躲进器官
茫然打着器官而你躲进狂想
漆黑的石柱打着大海　看清一声
"啊"　它新月般悬挂着复活

218

4

in Athens   the poet Patrokles groaned 'Enough'
the rain of 423 BC on these foreheads was enough
the neck of nightmare news snapped   marble nests
discarded on pine needles   pale festering thought enough
bulls on the altar wail and wail before slaughter
stimulating spring grass   the dead's bitter odour
for whom are the branches of a guidebook hung?
what solace can throats buried in megaphones bring?
in the orbits of the Greek tongue the ocean is a handful of dried
dust   too painful   don't torment the spirits of the dead

5

but your departed spirit wallows unquiet upon you
blue locked into your paddling like a peacock spreading its tail
higher than the cliffs   higher than history
crystal shimmer filling the weight crashes a drop of rain
one foetus in line with seven thousand auctioned slaves
lower than the sandstone path   lower still
weeping from below ground clutches at shuffling sandalled feet
you're carved as desperately looking out to serve your time in jail
blue far away as home   seabed endlessly sunk in vice
a raindrop falling a thousand years still hasn't touched your face

6

a shower of Syracusan rain has muddled time
fallen in books   fallen with the cold of composed style
in your eyes there is always the shifting carved windowsill
carrying the scarlet-soaked roses on top of the wall
in your face the topless women walk on by
dilapidated words leave a lump of shy flesh unlocked
time is pounding skin and you hide inside your viscera
empty vastness is pounding viscera but you hide in mad fantasy
jet-black stone pillars are pounding the ocean   see clearly one
'oh'   it hangs out resurrection like a new moon

七

远眺发明几何学　女儿隐身瞧着
你脚下踢起的石头　一次死
翻开人的灰烬　一条石车辙堙入荒草
翻找一个耸立在暗处的字母
无声爆发的哭声进驻女祭司的火把
带你走过一条街　橙子树的香气
缝合血和沙　沉船和燕子　女儿
跳跳停停的心复述一篇演讲辞
另一个黄昏从地貌中拧出紫色
书边滑落的手指　轻易掠走一切

八

就这样拨动大理石起伏的海涛
就这样房间里雨声彻夜响
挽歌　挽着女儿怕出生的性
就这样岸夹紧噩耗滚烫的钳子
灯下读到一支大军走投无路
宿营的篝火倒映仔细策划的
仔细忘却的　云和风的圆形剧场
录制婴孩身上嚎啕的蜜蜡色
活是一次看不见的展示　她
来过　手中牵着一大群消失

九

每个词都在不该在的地方　怀揣
自己的裂缝　每个词汪着眼泪
不流　才描出早已流尽的干枯
每张石头脸颊下建造着石牢
偷听刀砍似的爱　不该滋生的爱
你身上的裂缝不该蔓延时蔓延
到海上　再次孵化成有张小脸的
蓝　拍打一首刚刚入睡的诗
每个词在雪白折页间亮晶晶的
该结束偏偏成为你开始的理由

220

7

gazing into the distance discovers geometry   daughter secretly watches
the stones your feet kick up   dying once
to open and read human ashes   stone ruts hop back into the weeds
to discover the alphabet of a place secretly soaring to the sky
silently exploding tears garrison the Bacchantes' torches
take you walking by a street   fragrance of orange trees
sews up blood and sand   sunken ships and swallows   daughter
leaping and stopping heart retells the words of a lecture
another twilight twists purple from the terrain
fingers sliding from a book   easily steal everything away

8

just so churns the rise and fall of the marble ocean's swell
just so in the room through the night the rain's sound
a dirge   holds the sex of a daughter afraid to be born
just so the scalding forceps of nightmare news clasped by the strand
reading by lamplight of a great army checkmated
garrison campfires reflecting the carefully-planned
carefully-forgotten   theatre-in-the-round of clouds and wind
recording the infant body's bawling beeswax colour
living is a one-off unseen revelation   she
once came   hands dragging a host of the vanished

9

every word is in a place it shouldn't be   holding
its own fissures   each word filled with tears   unflowing
then they trace a long flowed-away shrivelling
build a stone jail beneath every stone cheek
overhearing love like a knife-wound   love that should not breed
cracks on your body spread when they shouldn't
to out at sea   they hatch over and again into a little face's
blue   slap a poem that has just fallen asleep
each word between the snow-white page-folds glittering
what should have been an end becomes just the reason for your beginning

十

每一百三十六天大海裂开一次
雨滴的小孔中能窥见白白的卵
选用这周期　荡漾的血味儿
不让你心里那道悬崖安息
选用一只射穿风景的海鸥
像个滚着花边扑上码头的女孩
劫掠父亲　锡拉库札窗台下
每一百三十六天大海停顿一次
搦住　又松开　不可能的呼吸
无限冷的雨声终究无限温柔

10

each hundred and thirty-six days the sea splits open
white eggs visible in the raindrops' alveoli
select this cycle   the rippling taste of blood
won't let the precipice in your heart rest in peace
select a seagull shooting through the scenery
like a girl rolling lace to pounce on the jetty
robbing father   below the windowsills of Syracuse
once each hundred and thirty six days the ocean will pause
discard   relax again   an impossible breathing
in the end the sound of infinitely cold rain is infinitely soft

一次石雕上手提净瓶的漫步

废墟浮上嘴角　　一首诗
续写石头的信　　一根食指
钩住不奢望寄走的水声

阳光暴晒的山坡上
你腋窝酥软　　忘了闲置过
第几个向海行走的一千年

你雪白的瓶子里盛满了铀
第几次倒空被发明的海
浑身血脉盯着那瓶口

变得更美　　为对抗那瓶口
刺眼的蓝等在大理石柱廊尽头
激情的残疾　　来　　毁了再来

一首诗怀着裂变亭亭玉立
一串幽暗的心跳像脚印
原地趟过　　恍若最后的

一步踏入石头的最初
半裸的肩膀下栖着燕子
飞来叫眼泪　　飞去叫欢快

你的爱仍然静静卡在正午
修饰你的爆炸　　玲珑地
提着所有的字

A walk on carved stone with water-bottle in hand

ruins float to the corner of a mouth   a poem
keeps writing a stone letter   a forefinger
hooks the sound of water that has no hope of being sent away

on sun-scorched slopes
you armpits are languid   have forgotten they had been idle
how many millennia that walked to the sea

your snow-white bottle is filled with uranium
how many times emptied out by an invented sea
every vein in your body staring at the bottle's mouth

turned lovelier   to resist the bottle's mouth
blinding blue waits at the end of a marble colonnade
deformity of passion   comes   after its ruin comes back

a poem embracing fission gracefully stands
a string of dark heartbeats like footprints
walk the same place   seemingly at the end

one step into stone's beginning
roosting swallows under half-naked shoulders
fly in named tears   fly out named joy

your love is still silently stuck at noon
decorating your explosion   exquisitely
lifting all the words

恍若雪的存在——完美之诗

整座雪山微微旋转　当你的脸
每秒钟更埋入诀别的幽暗
远离阳光像远离一场诬陷
说　你暂停过　爱过　雪映蓝天

有过置换的主题　继续玩味
你肉里吱吱叫的白色沙子
一片云玲珑寒意的袍子
水做的女道士　抹掉自己　恰似纵欲

水中拆毁的表情　亮晶晶聆听
冰川磨尖的爪子在爬动
一只苹果里盗墓者的洞
偷运死之甜　你的空茫　最后的激情

更醉心　雪花的拂尘
拂拭一个没有你的早晨
雪白的麻鞋踩出雪线那行脚印
更高　鹰叼起人类的肠子　啄碎的心

不怕总在路上　你的狂想
剥离你生存的形象
听　器官慢慢说谎
编造　雪崩的辞　越落不到地面越嚣张

白茫茫的虚构　照耀你的结构
冷晶莹绽开在你身后
发育雪的绕指柔
毁啊　一首诗平行于怒云　烟岚　湍流

都是变的　一杯茶的漩涡
搅动那么多海拔那么多
记住的　却并非你的干渴
一滴墨不是蓝色　不是黑色　是金色

226

Existence that seems snow – A perfect poem

the whole snowy mountain turns slightly   as your face
is buried deeper each second in the gloom of a last goodbye
far away from the sunlight as if far away from a frame-up
say   you stopped a while   loved   snow reflecting blue sky

there was a replaced topic   continuing to relish
the chirruping of white sand in your flesh
cloud cover a gown of finely-wrought cold
Taoist priestess made of water   rubbing herself out   like a debauch

a look demolished in water   listens sparkling
claws ground sharp by glaciers crawling
a tomb-robber's cave inside an apple
smuggles the sweetness of death   your vast void   last craving

more enthralled   the snowflakes' whisking horsetail
gently wipes a morning without you
on the snowline snow-white sandals step a footprint trail
higher up   an eagle's beak lifts human guts   a heart pecked apart

don't fear being always on the road   your crazy delusions
peel off the image of your existence
listen to   viscera slowly uttering deceptions
concocting   the avalanche's words   the wilder they are the less they can fall

a vast whiteness of fabrication   lights up your construction
cold bursts in crystal after you pass by
to grow snow's soft sinuousity
oh destruction   a poem parallel to angry cloud   mountain mist   inundation

all is change   in a tea cup a whirlpool
stirs so many sea-levels so much to recall
thirst   but certainly not yours
an ink-drop isn't blue   it isn't black   it's gold

书写名字的大雪
你滑坠的草坡无限阴绿
你手上的绷带一直湿漉漉缠着
一场跋涉　置换成记忆　不奢望终结

知道　水之道
就是洗净肌肤　把美准备好
放弃给你爱的　那高潮
哪管渗漏的是谁　缨络　纷纷洒扫

把覆盖你的白　炼制为
此刻暴露你的白
递增非人的完美
说　恍若　仅仅恍若　雪的　存在

writing the snowstorm of names
you slide down endless grey-green grassy slopes
bandages on your hands a wet torment
a long hike   displaced into a memory   to end no high hopes

know a Tao   the Tao of water
is washed-clean skin   beauty all preparation
to give itself up to what you love   that high tide
who cares who was leaked?   pearl necklaces   swept away in succession

the white that covers you   refined
into the white that in this moment reveals you
grow by degrees into inhuman excellence
speak   seemingly   only seemingly   snow's   existence

思想面具（一）

必须拧亮那盏灯　让侧光
斜射进摒住呼吸的白
一块石膏里溺死的白

必须复活于影子
斜斜描摹一场被驱逐的雪
驱逐进房间里　你的安详

有呛人的味儿　捏制一枚
尖尖拱出平面的精巧的鼻子
嗅着乡愁　最香的暮色

从死鱼一边稳稳升起
像座迫使绿色海浪显形的航标
打湿一盆盆全速航行的花草

照耀眼睛只为刺瞎眼睛
钙化的耳朵一举省略掉耳朵
一张脸内脏般藏起思想

把深陷的　易碎的窗口
挂在霜红的枝叶间　拆散人生
那洇开的依托着空气的花朵

Thinking mask 1

it is necessary to switch the lamp on   to let the sidelight
shine aslant into the white of its held breath
the white of drowning in a lump of plaster

it is necessary to be reborn in shadow
to be obliquely tracing a banished snowfall
banished to a room   your serenity

there is a taste of choking   kneaded into
a finely-wrought sharp nose sprouting from a level plane
smelling homesickness   a most perfumed dusk

rising steadily from beside the dead fish
like a buoy forcing the green waves to reveal themselves
watering flowerpots sail full speed ahead

light up the eyes only to blind the eyes
once-calcified ears ignore the ears
like viscera a face hides thoughts

hang the deep-sunk   brittle windows
among the branches of the frost-red vine   break life apart
that feathering flower that relies on air

思想面具（二）

世界为影子忙碌　雕刀
刮掉墙上水蜜桃娇艳的颜色
给灯笼安进火苗

一边是减法　关掉星期天
作品就在阳光中剜出空洞
一边相加　成群的黄蜂

蜇疼成群冷凝在石膏上的
肮脏指纹　你潜藏的影子
逼你发育肉　颧骨　牙　躯体

一边坍塌在无情地构思
一边堆积尖叫　石质的神经
再崩裂就成了无声的　你

低垂眼帘　谨守墙的秘密
守着自己震耳欲聋的心跳
什么也不说　像利刃

于是语言辉煌地说出
一件雕塑无限趋近人形的
不真实的美

Thinking mask 2

the world is busy with shadows   the carver's knife
scrapes away the tender colours of the honey-peaches on the walls
fits the lamps with flame

subtract on the one hand   Sunday switched off
a work of art gouges a hole in the sunlight
add on the other   the wasps swarming

painful stings in swarms of dirty fingerprints
condensed on plaster   your hidden shadow
forces you to grow flesh   cheekbones   teeth   carcass

collapse on one hand in a callously-plotted tale
on the other pile screams up   stone-natured nerves
burst open again to become silence   you

lower your eyes   keep the wall's secret safe
guard your own thunderous heartbeat
say not a thing   like a keen blade

so language speaks gloriously out
a sculpture of endlessly approaching human forms
an untruthful beauty

思想面具（三）

漆黑的羽毛把翱翔变成静物
面具刷新你和我的猖狂
戴着说　自由　但是假的

诗句　制作一个燕子们的下午
眼睛　盯着黑手套托起柠檬
明媚是一种公共的耻辱

戴着说　歧途　但酷爱着
蓝色清洁剂清除的鸟儿的残迹
两个人之间唯有爱的歧途

能映照彼此　把自己
虐待进孤独的天堂里去　观赏
一阵呼啸中沦为静物的北风

戴着落叶与河水　说
测量一场天边积蓄的大雪
用内心珍藏的黑暗彼此对位吧

倒扣在无所不在的墙上
一堆羽毛慢慢腐烂　耳鸣中
一座鸟鸣博物馆象征地活着

Thinking mask 3

jet-black feathers turn hovering into still life
the mask refreshes your madness and mine
wearing it say   freedom   but it's not true

a verse   creates an afternoon of swallows
eyes   gaze at black gloves lifting a lemon
glamour is a kind of shared shame

wearing it say   wrong road   but loving passionately
the traces of birds eliminated by blue detergent
between two people there is only the wrong road of love

can reflect each of them   torture
yourself into a lonely heaven   watch the view of
a whistling blast of north wind reduced to a still life

wearing fallen leaves and river water   speak
measure a great snowfall piled at the sky's edge
counterpoint each other with darkness carefully hoarded in our inmost hearts

upside down on the omnipresent wall
a pile of slowly rotting feathers   in tinnitus
a museum of birdsong symbolically alive

思想面具 （四）

死海豚侧着眼张望人的镜头
一枚清澈的小黑窟窿　好奇
借来的存在多么放肆

借来五颜六色的盐的几何学
雕一朵大教堂的奇花
雕出的脚步　粘进咸咸的甬道

一股嗅觉像鬼火引我们游荡
一对腌制的性别固定大海
肉欲的　保鲜的性质

唯一该问　还有人能问吗？
当月光也像谎言的矿物被开采着
当谎言　已成熟为一种激情了

唯一该感到那只死海豚
仍按在岩层里　拍打　某张脸
自幽深处喷出雪白的雾气

满房间失重的瓷器　尾随
你胸前甜蜜摇荡的导航仪
一路碎裂声正是谢幕的艺术

Thinking mask 4

a dead dolphin looks sideways to peer into the human camera lens
a tiny little limpid black cavity   curious
borrowed existence so wanton

borrowing the colourful geometry of salt
to carve a rare flower of a cathedral
carving out footsteps   stuck in a salty tomb corridor

smell of something like wildfire leads us to loiter
a pair of pickled sexes fix in place the ocean's
nature of desire   preserved fresh

the only question that should be asked   is anyone able to question?
as moonlight is like a mendacious mineral extracted
so mendacity   has matured into passion

the only way to feel should be on that dead dolphin
left still in rock strata   slap   some face
spitting out a snow white mist from a place of deep silence

weightless porcelain fills the room   following after
your breast's sweetly swaying navigation
disintegration's sound has always been the art of the curtain call

思想面具（五）

返回蝴蝶般精巧扇动的鼻翼
嗅　空气中持续赋予
持续散开的形式

返回一只花园中翻飞的老虎
穿上它不认识的名字
世界就绘满金黄的斑纹

涓涓流去时也涓涓流回
你不认识陶土的形式
却认出一只埙酿造千年的醉意

那翅膀的形式　落进落日
敷到嘴唇上的深紫色　蝴蝶
认出杜甫吧　够惨痛　必须够美丽

脸的形式　遭遇
一只鸟俯冲的形式　高高挑起
黑　蓝　绿　被激怒的羽毛

一阵毛茸茸的语法中
愤怒的花朵赢得了大选
爱只爱消溶在纯粹道德中的你

Thinking mask 5

return to nostrils finely-wrought and flapping like a butterfly
sniff   continually presenting
continually scattered shapes in the air

return to a tiger fluttering in a flower garden
wearing a name it doesn't recognise
so the world is painted over with yellow-gold stripes

when they trickle away they trickle back too
you don't recognise the shape of clay
but you do know drunkenness brewed a thousand years by the ocarina

the shape of those wings   setting into the setting sun
deep purple smeared on the lips   butterfly
please recognise Du Fu   unbearable enough   must be lovely enough

a face's shape encounters
the shape of a diving bird   provoking from on high
infuriated   black   blue   green   feathers

in that feathery grammar
enraged flowers have won the election
the only love is to love the you that melts in unalloyed virtue

思想面具（六）

窗口的造型鲜明如造物
嵌着一阵扫射玻璃的冷雨
嵌着站在窗台上摇摇欲坠的孩子

都是面具　石膏的玄思
用影子逼你现身　你
拧亮斜射的灯逼黑暗现身

肯定一场雪盲症　不停
把窗外弥漫的景致移到窗内
孩子绷紧的粉红色地平线

浸透不可能更空的奶味儿
喂养纷纷洒落的家庭的粉末
鲜嫩的脸涤净至零

什么也没做　世界已经变了
一块雪白的平面外无需别的葬礼
留给杰作的只是芳香

这房间悬在到处的海底
听见孩子的月光嘎嘎开裂
每一夜被抚摸成虚拟的石头

Thinking mask 6

the window moulding bright as Creation
inlaid with cold rain bombarding the glass
inlaid with a child teetering on the windowsill

all masks   mysticisms of plaster
use shadows to make you show yourself   you
switch on the slanting lamp to make darkness show itself

confirming a case of snow blindness   endlessly
moving the outside view that fills the window to inside the window
a pink horizon children have tightened

soaked in a milky taste that couldn't be emptier
feeds the families' powder sprinkled everywhere
a fresh and tender face cleaned into a zero

and nothing done   the world has changed
no need for another funeral except one flat plane
what's left of the masterpiece is only an aroma

this room hangs on a seabed that is everywhere
hearing the child's moonlight crackle and split
stroked every single night into a made-up stone

鬼魂作曲家——自白

一切始于一次性交
当日子不多不少是一场剥光的仪式
当一个人剥光得连年龄也不剩
乐曲　直指子宫里的嫩

血红压低的穹顶　忍着一枝蕊
既像梅花又像槐花
没完没了扫得你爆炸

　　我藏在手指背后　音符背后
　　弹起　又按下一枚水鸟的琴键
　　拆卸光年的机器

　　我藏在一个过不去的昨夜背后
　　听　黑暗追问一道狂暴推移的极限

全部乐谱只等待一盏灯
支起望远镜　细细勘测一张旧照
翻开相册的时候就是知道
你不会回来的时候　而抚摸
贴紧毁灭已经发生的心境
透视白的下颌　白的眉骨　白的唇
一个家庭在射线中繁衍成负数
最色情时子宫彻夜醒着　吻合
我贯穿星际的秘密爱你的仪式

　　我藏进演奏寂静的力　擎着大海
　　想怎么蓝就怎么蓝的形状
　　噩耗想怎么扩散就怎么扩散

全部黄昏的房间总是相册里
最后写满　最后撕下的那一页
童年的口音掏空扔过窗口的云

Ghost composer – Confession

everything began from one sex act
as days neither many nor few are a stripped-bare ritual
as a person is stripped so naked even age is not left
music   points only to the tenderness in the womb

dome of falling blood-red   suffering one stamen
is like blossoms of plum or pagoda tree
endlessly swept until you explode

    I hide behind my fingers   behind musical notes
    pluck   and press a water-bird piano key
    dismantle a machine of light-years

    I hide behind a yesterday's night that cannot pass
    hear   darkness question a frantically-expiring limit

the full musical score waits only for a lamp
to support the telescope   to explore an old photo with great care
when you flick through the album is when you know
you can't come back   and touch
a mood stuck tightly to destruction that has already happened
x-ray white jawbone   white brow ridge   white lips
in the rays a family multiplying into a negative number
at its lewdest moment the womb is awake all night   to fit
my star-penetrating ritual of loving you in secret

    I hide in the power to perform silence   lifting the ocean
    a form as blue as it wants to be
    nightmare news spread as wide as it wants to be

the whole twilight room   is always in the album
the last page written   the last page torn out
childhood's spendthrift accent threw away the window clouds

相爱的口音淋湿抓紧地面的落叶
每条街带着自己的口音　　加入
行走　　被放弃的死者使一个梦更嘈杂
你坐在幽暗中听　　清　　疼痛
那不能分解的化学向内卷曲
一枝梅花艳艳涂写
一枝槐花瞪视漏下的明月

　　　没别的结构除了声音之间的停顿
　　　比声音更刺耳　　没别的宇宙
　　　除了锁在皮肤下索索发抖的大爆炸
　　　听觉加速时　　躯体无限推迟
　　　我藏进一次黑暗中绝望的射精

　　　射入假想成胎儿的现实
　　　从未真的存在因而加倍剥夺你
　　　没别的调性除了彻底抹平的肺活量
　　　像个墓碑上移动的字
　　　彻底　　呈现被向往的哑默

the drenched accent of love clutches fallen leaves on the ground
every street brings its own accent   to join
walking   the abandoned dead make a dream deafening
you sit in the dark hearing   clear   pain
that unresolvable chemistry curling inwards
a branch of plum blossom opulently scrawling
a branch of plum blossom gazing at the bright leaking moon

     no other structure but pauses between sounds
     more piercing than sound   no other universe
     but a great locked explosion shuddering beneath the skin
     when hearing speeds up   the body is endlessly put off
     I hide in a despairing ejaculation in the dark

     shoot into the reality of an imagined fully-formed foetus
     so doubly depriving you of a not yet real existence
     no other mode but smeared and entirely flat-lined
     like letters moving on gravestones
     comprehensively   manifesting as total and long yearned-for silence

一件事

仅仅一件　在回头看的眼睛里
仅仅一片茫茫　却
遮住一瓶酒摇出的风景

你跳伞到爸爸门口时　一百公里高空
冷凝的叫卖声正摊开北极光
电视上雪橇疾驰　满载五颜六色的衬衫

你的衬衫里　五颜六色的火
放养一头怦怦跳荡顶撞青春的鹿

爸爸的室内北极光飘动
缤纷的冰雪坐在一起只感到那飘动

飘了一百年　回头还堵在尽头

某个血缘悬在针叶林上方　衔着
你的尾　蘸进夜里墨迹淋漓
你的角　嵌成天空的婴儿车
傻样的歌声把一顿晚餐还原为紫色
坚信听到北极光的响声
不分季节地说　别了

狼眼中霓虹粼粼的河水
不停拆下一块地平线的荧光屏

没人走出孩子这件事
敲定聋了的天文学那件事
模仿你傻笑　喷出五颜六色的哈气

One thing

only one thing   in eyes that look back
only one vast emptiness   yet
it blocks the scenery shaken out from the beer bottle

when you parachute into Dad's door   at a hundred kilometres up
the condensed cries of hawkers spread an aurora borealis
speeding sledges on TV   full of multicoloured shirts

inside your shirt   multicoloured fire
a deer whose thumping heartbeat head-butts youth

the aurora flutters and dances in Dad's room
helter-skelter snow and ice sit together feeling only that fluttering

has been fluttering for a century   looking back still blocked at the very end

certain blood ties hang on the heights of needled woods   between the teeth
your tail   dipped in night's ink-drenched handwriting
your horn   inset in the baby-carriage of the sky
silly songs return a dinner to its original purple
convinced the noise of the aurora is audible
irrespective of the season say   goodbye

crystal neon shining of water in the wolf's eye
endlessly dismantles the horizon of the TV screen

no one walks away from this child thing
to fix the deaf astronomy thing
copies your silly smile   belches a multicoloured sigh

一次叙述

你从不后悔蓦入错误
一种明晰一种美　词是错
无词　就再错一次　窗台
摆上一排悲鸣的雁　蓝的鞭子狠狠抽
空间那朵茶花

雕琢成洗劫的力　比负数中
玲珑的倒影更有力

李河谷沼泽的眼窝里一滴实心的泪
镀了月光　一块琥珀沉吟成人形
爱上爱情也爱上厌倦

迎着负星座　呼吸节拍器一次性作曲

什么不是书？又冷又亮
一把秋空的镰刀割下满地落叶
割掉山喜鹊跳来跳去的自恋

哪本书不是花瓣那本？飘零
就把你引渡进爸爸的泥泞那同一本？
浸染在风里　鱼腥味儿的负颜色
篡改哮喘的大海

听浪拍打　本来该这样
你写的不多不少粉碎成你是的
你是你的变幻　说出的都是真的
吸进肺里的雨仍深深下　越下欠得越多
压坠红艳的露珠　刷新被眺望的活
云　飘过茶花的内脏
发育成自己孤独的祖国

Once-told

you never regret walking into a mistake
a kind of clarity a kind of beauty   words are wrong
wordless   so wrong again   windowsill
set with a row of lamenting geese   blue whips ruthlessly budding
the camellia of the sky

carved into the power of looting   more powerful
than the tinkling reflection in a negative number

one honest teardrop in Lee Valley Marsh's eye sockets
has plated the moonlight   a lump of amber in its musing becomes a human shape
to fall in love with love and weariness too

facing the burden of constellations   breath's metronome writes a one-off tune

what is not a book?   cold and bright
the sickle of the autumn sky shears fallen leaves all around
shears away the narcissism of the magpies hopping to and fro

which book is not that book of petals?   did fading and falling
deport you to Dad's same muddy book?
in the contaminated winds   negative colours of a fishy stench
falsify an asthmatic ocean

hear the waves slap   it should originally be like this
what you write shatters into exactly what you are
you are your changes   all that is spoken is true
the rain you breath into your lungs still goes deep   the deeper down the more
                                                                        it owes
weighing down the blush-pink dewdrop   renewing a life surveyed
clouds   drifting pass the camellia's viscera
grow into your own lonely motherland

一抹颜色

噩梦中的人加速度迸发呼喊

这里的蓝想变就变黑　　这里
绿一刹那分解成金黄和银红
谁的奢华的意志　　拒绝你醒来

掼出你

这里的蛇皮像填满白垩的花园一样
蜕掉　　这里月光孵出一株水仙
颜色俯吻你　　颜色丢弃你

没人能摸到这世界时　　你床头歪着
童年　　像朵云重重砸在头上

噩梦中的人擅长最柔软的抒情

去抵消一生无色的化学
只要嗅　　海就是幸福的瞎子
只要听　　树枝就从天空到内心挂满哨音
这里没什么可背叛　　因为臆想就是颜色

松开你

一只狗眼中昏暗的影子始终真实
你两岁已画下一枚漏尽鲜血的水仙
锯齿形的早晨挣扎在蛹里

噩梦中的人像蝴蝶炸开自己

One touch of colour

someone in a nightmare breaks out in an accelerating cry

blue here can be black if it wants to change
green here disintegrates into rose-pink in an instant
someone's lavish willpower   refuses that you wake

tossing you out

snakeskin here is like a garden stuffed with chalk
sloughed off   here moonlight hatches a narcissus
colour bows down to kiss you   colour discards you

when no one can touch this world   your bedhead reclining
childhood   like a cloud heavily pounding your head

  someone in a nightmare is expert in the gentlest lyric

to offset your lifelong colourless chemistry
you need only smell   so the sea is happily blind
you need only hear   so from sky to inmost heart branches are all hung with
                                                                    whistling
nothing here can be betrayed   because supposition is colour

releasing you

dim shadows in a dog's eye have always been real
at two you had already drawn a narcissus leaked dry of blood
a saw-toothed morning struggling in the chrysalis

someone in a nightmare is like a butterfly blasting itself apart

一种声音

听女道士柔柔的笺揉碎你的桃花
听井汲取火　说自己的方言

名字里的墨　滴进雾散后那滴墨
星星的音乐会加上回声的纵深

你一转身隐入天边的象征

把接吻留给背后黑黝黝的小旅馆
重播的孤独拨动七根弦的世界
流星的逍遥似曾相识

把舌头温柔地顶进耳鼓　这峭崖
录制耳鸣锐利的　伫立的频率
消散的诗意　一艘飞船

无生命的字骑上星座改变你的生命

那首渐渐长成的爱情诗
呼吸着此刻总过于清冽的大气
一片被唤作墨的夜空堆满了雪
一场雪剑一样抽出　吟诵中
剑锋抖落覆盖群山的晶莹的粉末

没别的方言除了爱　刚刚做的
渗出泪　翻过又一年

又凭空辨认出　从远方荡回的
同一次高潮迸发的喊声

One kind of sound

hear the Taoist priestess's gentle paper crumbling your peach blossom
hear the well draw up fire   speaking its own dialect

ink in names   drips into ink drops once mist has dispersed
a concert of stars added to an echo's depth

you turn round then hide in a symbol at the ends of the earth

leave a kiss for the dark hotel behind you
re-broadcast aloneness strums a seven-string world
you seem to have met free-as-air meteors before

push your tongue gently in to an eardrum   this precipice
records tinnitus's ear-piercing   long-frozen frequency
dispersed poetics   a spaceship

lifeless letters riding constellations change your life

the love poem that gradually grows up
breathing this instant an always too chill atmosphere
a slice of night sky called ink piled up with snow
a fall of snow drawn out like a sword   in recitation
the blade shakes off the crystal powder that covers the mountains

no other dialect but love   newly made
leaking tears   turn over another year

recognise again out of nothing   swaying back from far away
a rising cry of simultaneous orgasm

一点倒影

母亲死后三十三年才生出惊人的美
你书桌上小小的蜡烛在送信
小小的祭坛用黑暗为她描眉

烛光摇摇欲坠了三小时
一张脸嵌进金鹧鸪　笑看房间
圣家族挪用的三小时

血肉微微浑浊的空气中疾驰而过
历史借走的　夜色还回的

绿油油的水仙旁她仍埋头织着毛衣
三十三年　针本身拧成死结
一间记忆的温室测不出温度
金鹧鸪冻僵的金色　打造娇嗔的首饰

佩带在黑暗上　借一盏烛台梳妆
谁全然冷漠才陪你共同度过时间

让一个人更突出家的主题
让死亡像个新家　倒映挤坐着的
红颜　俯视你时剑刃一一劈下
母亲非物质的光慢慢图画到你脸上
抽象成三小时　痴痴潜入海底

每天的周年　你爱上那因为爱
已全然成为你自己的美

One drop of inverted reflection

Mother's amazing beauty only born thirty-three years after her death
little candles on your desk deliver letters
the tiny altar pencils her brows with darkness

candlelight's flicker tottering for three hours
a face inlaid in a golden francolin   looks at the room with a smile
three hours misappropriated by the Holy Family

in the faintly dirty air flesh and blood gallop past
what history borrows   what night gives back

beside fresh green narcissus her head is bowed over the sweater she knits
thirty-three years   needles twisting themselves into a granny knot
 a hothouse of memory can't fathom temperature
the frozen-stiff gold of a golden francolin   makes petulant jewellery

wear it in the dark   dress and make up by a borrowed lamp
only someone utterly cold will share time with you

let a man stress the subject of family more
let death resemble a new home   reflecting close-sitting
rosy cheeks   when they're bending over you a sword blade   sunders blow
                                                                    by blow
mother's immaterial light slowly painted on your face
abstracted into three hours   sinking idiotically to the seabed

on the daily anniversary   you fall in love with what because of love
has become a beauty entirely your own

空书——火中满溢之书

每一刹那是一张簇新的白纸
许多年　一个漫长移动的句子
写下了什么？你是一根铜弦
揉啊　幽咽中投入火的手指
贴近审视宇宙那撤走的宴席
唱和着什么？一部组装的音乐
组装出寂静　火舌明艳地指挥

　　你脸颊上的温度　你的心跳
　　暴露咽喉下死过两次的月色
　　如雪坍塌　如乱伦的幸福的征兆

你的知音就在一行诗句中藏着
火　自焚的玫瑰　总定格
于将将烫伤时　将将在手边
嗅到历史的焦糊　烟袅袅拂过
擦拭一个人里无数人的天际
无数水面是一本书　玫瑰色
被天鹅溅落的脚蹼装订成暮色

　　一只青瓷天球瓶宁静又狂暴
　　用波浪形的耳廓盛满聆听
　　你的扬扬挥洒　你咳嗽的同谋

相遇　在一抹流水上命名
相忘　你们彼此为焰　为镜
为期待　拈出一枚深怀的蕊
墨汁做的半人半鬼的空
无论多远都让你们拥抱取暖
瘦瘦的火中　每首诗将将开屏
完成一只孔雀震颤的表情

Empty book – Book brimming with fire

it's a brand-new sheet of white paper every instant
many years   an endlessly-moving sentence
what's written down?   you are a brass string
oh rub   fingers thrown in the fire amid whimpering
stuck to observing that withdrawing feast the universe
what is sung in chorus?   a piece of constructed music
constructing silence   tongues of flame shiningly conducting

     temperature on your cheek   your heartbeat
     lay bare moonlight twice-dead beneath your throat
     like an avalanche   like incest's lucky portent

your soul-mate is hidden in a line of verse
fire   self-immolating rose   always freezes the frame
when barely scalding   barely at hand
the burning smell of history   flicked away in curling smoke
wipe the skyline clean of the countless people in one person
countless waters are a book   with rose-pink colouring
bound into dusk by the swans' webs paddling

     a celadon globe-vase both tranquil and intemperate
     an auditory sense filled with ears all wave-shaped
     your floating in the air   your coughing confederate

encounter   naming on a smear of running water
forget   you are flame for each other   are a mirror
an expectation   pluck out one tiny deeply-cherished stamen
an ink emptiness is half-man half-ghost
no matter how far it makes you huddle together for warmth
in the thin thin fire   each poem barely spreads its train
to perfect the peacock's quivering features

烛照　一根琴弦上俯身的韵脚
向日葵金黄撕碎的语言
毁得美一点　唯一的必要

唯一的倒计时只演奏一种思念
给谁呢？一首挽歌中满满
溢出这人称　借用你的第一天
一个炼字　提纯可怕的界限
反复熔铸的词性肯定更可怕的无限
唱着血肉　唱着灰烬　黑得不做梦
炼　亲密约定最后一天

　　两次来到
　　洗劫后的洁净　月光的幽咽
　　缕缕幽香　让你听你在逍遥

2005-2009

258

illuminate   a rhyme bowed down over one string
sunflower's golden language shredded
a little more beautifully destroyed   the one and only necessity

the one and only countdown merely performs a kind of longing
who for?   a dirge full of
overflowing personal pronouns   borrows your first day
an alchemical word   refines a terrifying end
repetitively-wrought linguistic nature confirms a more terrifying endlessness
sing flesh and blood   sing ashes   black enough to be dreamless
forge   an intimately-arranged last day

twice arrived-at
post-looted cleanness   moonlight's whimper
wafts of faint perfume   let you hear you are free as the air

2005-2009

Ghost Composer / Ghost Translator

Yang Lian's «敘事詩» *Xùshìshī*, or *Narrative Poem*, is his most personal work to date, built as it is around a series of family photographs, the first of which was taken on the day that he was born on February 20th, 1955, and the last of which dates from 1974 to 1977, a period he spent in Changping county near Beijing to undergo 're-education through labour', and where he did various labouring jobs, including digging graves. The poetry ranges backward and forward in time, covering the poet's childhood and youth, his exile in New Zealand, where he married his wife YoYo (Liu Youhong), his subsequent adventures and travels in and around Europe and elsewhere, as well as meditations on time, consciousness, history and memory.

Narrative Poem uses rhyme much more extensively than any previous book of Yang's, which presents a specific set of challenges for the translator: Chinese rhymes with much greater facility than English does. Modern Standard Chinese has many fewer speech sounds than English, and can happily continue one rhyme over many lines, so, with the best will in the world, it is not going to be possible to replicate in translation every rhyme scheme a Chinese poet uses.

Yang's rhyming is elegant and creative, and, while it is aware of the classical tradition, it is also innovative, making use of half-rhymes which would not, I suspect, have been allowed if the classical rules of Chinese prosody had been more strictly applied. That makes my job somewhat less difficult, in that it gives me licence to make use of half-rhymes too, as well as alliteration and other echoic devices that are not quite rhyme. I also take the chance to insert slant-rhymes here and there to compensate for end-rhymes I have not managed to replicate. If you see English rhymes, no matter how fragmentary, how limping, or how faint, then you may be sure there are rhymes in the Chinese text. Equally, unrhymed blank verse in English is a sign that, with a few short exceptions where I failed to find rhyme-words that would transmit the sense of Yang's text, the Chinese is also unrhymed.

The French poet Paul Valéry famously said, 'A poem is never finished: it is simply abandoned.' This is also the case with literary translation, and especially with translating poetry. There is no end to the improvements that could be made to a draft version – I have often returned again and again to an obstinate poem that will not work itself out for me, sometimes for years on end. And all writers and translators know the feeling of opening a new book for the very first time, only to discover a silly typo, or a problem whose solution we failed to see before. When I was an undergraduate at Edinburgh, I was lucky enough to study classical Chinese poetry with the inspiring, brilliant, and infuriating John Scott. The day he brought his first copy of *Poems of Love and Protest*[35] to class, we four students read some poems with him, and in Li Bai's To His Wife, where John rendered 泥醉 *nízuì* as '*drunk as mud*' I said (and how I wish I had bitten my tongue), 'Wouldn't it be better to say *plastered?*' John's face fell. An undergraduate had seen a solution that he hadn't. Well, in thirty-odd years of teaching, the same thing has happened to me many times, so I know now exactly how he must have felt.[36]

Yang Lian's poetry is neither easily approached nor easily understood. As the Scottish poet Gawin Douglas said in his superb translation of Virgil's *Aeneid* which he completed in 1513,

Consider it warly, reid oftar than anys
Weill at a blenk sle poetry nocht tayn is.[37]

Yang Lian and only I reach a provisionally "final" text after I have

---

35. John Scott and Graham Martin, *Poems of Love and Protest: Chinese Poems from the 6th Century BC to the 17th Century AD* (London: Rapp & Whiting, 1972). See p 72.

36. 泥醉 nízuì: 泥 ní 'mud, plaster'; 醉 zuì 'drunk'. Between the renderings 'drunk as mud' and 'plastered' lie two entire philosophies of translation, of course.

37. *Consider it carefully, read oftener than once / Clever poetry is not properly taken in at one look: Eneados, Prologue*, 108-9.

revised my early drafts with the aid of his commentaries and observations, and rewritten those drafts to insert rhymes where possible or necessary: then, when Yang checks through my last revisions to ensure that I have not drifted too far from the sense of his poetry while I am adding rhymes, we arrive at some kind of consensus on the best way for me to render the poems in English, in which I get the final word. It is a joy to work with a poet who understands the translator's predicament, and Yang is unfailingly helpful in his comments on my drafts: though he is not my co-translator, he certainly helps me a great deal with editing and revising, for which I am grateful.

In his preface, Yang has outlined the personal manifesto that underlies and is interwoven through his poetics, and, while respecting the translator's usual silence on such matters, I should now like to note some points that underlie the translator's traditional invisibility.

There is an abnegation of self involved in literary translation: it is not my voice the readers expect to be hearing, but the poet's. However, unless the reader has learned Chinese, it is of course my voice and only my voice that is audible, so I must make an effort to vanish, to channel the voice of Yang Lian and let him speak in English, and it is this ventriloquism, this speaking in tongues, that is at the heart of our paradoxical trade. He must be both visible and – in my imagined re-creation of his voice – audible, while I must remain invisible.

And yet I am here, and expect to be paid good cash money, expect to have my name emblazoned on the book beside Yang Lian's. When reviewers with no Chinese praise or dispraise Yang's poetry, what they are actually reviewing is my language, my metrics, my music, but his narrative and his images. If prizes are given out, do they go equally to the poet and the translator? Should they? Is my art a mere handmaiden of his? Traditional though it may be to hail the Apollonian generative power of the poetic sun at the expense of that pale lunar reflection, that sub-standard cover version, which is the best that the poor drudge of a translator is reckoned to be capable of, I would suggest – oh, the thrill of the British imperative! – that we should be giving consideration to equal treatment for both: just as Benjamin Britten gets the credit for reworking a cello suite by J.S. Bach, or Miles Davis is praised for reframing a piece by Rodrigo, why shouldn't the translated poem be acclaimed as an artifact whose beauty and value equal the original?

This assumes, of course, that the translator has, at the very least, sufficient skill and cunning to devise a seeming replica that will convincingly pass as a living poem – and that is not something to be lightly assumed.

The education of translators has changed beyond recognition in my lifetime: when I graduated from Edinburgh University in 1975, had there been such a thing as a postgraduate degree in the translation of Chinese, I would have jumped at it, but there was not. First at Larbert High School and then at Galashiels Academy, I would translate a passage from English into Latin and another from Latin to English, one into French and another from French, and for the last three or four years an additional one into Greek and another from Greek, so that, latterly, I was doing six translations every week – yet I do not recall any teacher ever sitting down and explaining what translation was, and how to do it. 'Construe, boy!' was the whole of the law. When I went to university to study Chinese, my teachers had been taught by the grammar-translation method, as all students had from time immemorial, and though they were keen to free themselves of it by using the newer communicative methods, translation remained the major classroom activity, and the main means of assessment. John Scott, Bill Dolby, and Dou Daoming were inspiring teachers, but the fact remains that, though I have been a published translator for thirty-five years, and was a teacher of translation for more than twenty years, I have never sat in a translation class as a student. I learned to translate by translating. It was the only way.

Modern translation courses cannot, of course, make a translator out of a tin-eared duffer, no matter how much computer assistance is provided, but they can and do speed up the entry into usefulness of the apprentice translator. And the astonishing range of software now available to facilitate the process of translation is a boon and a blessing to the harried professional. How wonderful it is to live in a small country town, as I do, almost forty miles from a reference library, and yet have access to almost all the dictionaries and reference works I need – but, children, if your tools are exclusively electronic, then you will miss the many great works of scholarship that have not yet been (and may never be) digitised, you will miss the joy of wandering the library's stacks to learn their unique geography, miss the intervention of the Library Angel who puts into your line of sight the misfiled book you didn't know you needed, miss the musty smell of old paper and glue and the crackle of a binding that hasn't been opened in years, miss the wholesome and nourishing silence of the reference room – you will forever miss, in short, the age-old full-body library experience that no virtual library can ever replicate.

There is still another parallel 'Narrative Poem', one yet to be written, which might relate a version of the translator's life, the secret life of that fugitive and preterite soul who speaks with someone else's tongue and thinks someone else's thoughts. In the meantime, overlaid on and interwoven with Yang Lian's «敘事詩» *Xùshìshī*, I have have given you *Narrative Poem*, which has tried to seduce you into believing that, as you picked your way through the ventriloquial labyrinth of my channelling of his Chinese, you have heard the resonance of Yang Lian's voice.

I am done speaking: now only you and Yang Lian haunt

this unseen structure   written by a ghost.

BRIAN HOLTON
Vienna, Melrose, Sliema
October 2015, revised February 2016, December 2016

TRANSLATOR'S ACKNOWLEDGEMENTS

I did some of the work on *Narrative Poem* as a 2014 Bogliasco Study Center Fellow, courtesy of the Bogliasco Foundation, and some as a Henry Luce Translation Fellow at Vermont Studio Center in 2014, and I would like to acknowledge my gratitude and my thanks to both organisations for the chance to work uninterrupted in surroundings of great beauty and collegiality. My especial thanks go to Ryan Walsh and his team at the the VSC for helping to make my stay so productive, and to Claudia, Alessandra, and the others at Villa dei Pini. Some poems appeared in issue 32 of *The Wolf* and in *Hwaet! 20 Years of Ledbury Poetry Festival* (Bloodaxe Books, 2016); others were presented at Poetry International Rotterdam 2013 and at StAnza 2013. Thanks also to Yang Lian for his unfailing generosity with his time.

This book has been selected to receive financial assistance from English PEN's Writers in Translation programme supported by Bloomberg and Arts Council England. English PEN exists to promote literature and its understanding, uphold writers' freedoms around the world, campaign against the persecution and imprisonment of writers for stating their views, and promote the friendly co-operation of writers and free exchange of ideas.

Each year, a dedicated committee of professionals selects books that are translated into English from a wide variety of foreign languages. We award grants to UK publishers to help translate, promote, market and champion these titles. Our aim is to celebrate books of outstanding literary quality, which have a clear link to the PEN charter and promote free speech and intercultural understanding.

In 2011, Writers in Translation's outstanding work and contribution to diversity in the UK literary scene was recognised by Arts Council England. English PEN was awarded a threefold increase in funding to develop its support for world writing in translation. www.englishpen.org